VIETNAM

Thai Dang Cao

OCTOPUS BOOKS

Acknowledgments

Editor: Diana Craig
Art Editor: David Rowley
Designer: Sue Storey
Copy Editor: Jenni Fleetwood
Production Controller: Trevor Jones

Special Photography: James Murphy
Food Preparation: Allyson Birch
Styling: Sarah Wiley
Illustrations: Paul Leith

The publishers wish to thank the following for providing photographs for this book:
C. Isy-Schwart/The Image Bank (page 5); the Hutchison Library (page 7)

Title page: Grilled Langoustine (page 23)

All recipes are for 4 servings unless otherwise stated
Vietnamese Green Salad (page 55) is taken from the *Encyclopaedia of Asian Cooking* and Beef and
Vegetable Salad (page 57) from *Oriental Cooking*

First published 1987 by
Octopus Books Limited
59 Grosvenor Street
London W1

ISBN 0 7064 3099 9

Printed in Hong Kong

Contents

VIETNAM

To cook Vietnamese food at home is perfectly simple and straightforward, as Thai-Dang-Cao's recipes in this book admirably illustrate. Thai-Dang-Cao was born and brought up in Saigon. The son of well-to-do parents, he learnt from an early age to eat well. As proprietor of several Vietnamese restaurants in London since leaving Vietnam, he has become used to cooking and serving authentic Vietnamese food outside his native land and has learnt first hand to strive for and attain authenticity. In this, his first book, he passes on this wealth of culinary experience and expertise. He introduces the reader gently to the art of Vietnamese cooking, to the dishes that are eaten daily by the majority of the Vietnamese people, particularly in the south where cooking is quick and simple and makes best use of the freshest possible ingredients.

It is a popular yet misconceived notion that Vietnamese and Chinese food are one and the same. In this book Thai-Dang-Cao sets out to dispel the myth. Similarities obviously exist because the Chinese ruled over Vietnam for more than 1000 years and therefore their influence was felt in the local cuisine, but Vietnamese food has very much its own character and flavour. In essence, Vietnamese food is a mixture and a refinement of many different cuisines – Thai, Indonesian, Indian and Cantonese with distinct French overtones – making it quite unique amongst the cuisines of the Orient. It is the perfect food for the modern, health-conscious diet of today.

Right: Vietnamese fisherman cast their nets

Culture and cuisine

It is a surprising fact that despite years of struggle against invasion by foreign powers, the Vietnamese have retained a distinct and sophisticated identity with their own culture, language, folklore, customs and, above all, cuisine. The Vietnamese culture is an ancient one, dating back more than 4000 years. From extensive archaeological research, scholars now believe that it was the Chinese and the Indians who learnt from the Vietnamese rather than the other way round as was previously thought, and that rice was harvested in Vietnam long before it was ever known in India or China.

The regions and their differences

Geographically, Vietnam is divided into three distinct regions, each with its own cuisine. The eastern seaboard of Vietnam covers 1400 miles of coastline, providing each of the three regions with an abundance of fish and shellfish. Rivers too are numerous, thus making Vietnam more of a fish-eating than a meat-eating nation as a whole. Rice is the staple food in all three regions and a dish of rice forms the central part of every meal, as in most south-east Asian countries.

North Vietnamese cooking is more obviously influenced by the neighbouring Chinese. Stir-frying is the most common cooking method and the north Vietnamese curries are sweet and mild like the Chinese. The Red River and its delta provide an abundance of fish, plus fertile, low-lying country for crops and pefect paddy fields for rice, but the climate is cooler in the north than in the centre and south, and therefore there is less choice of exotic fruits and vegetables. Northern cooking has the most sumptuous style of the three Vietnamese cuisines and is sometimes described as 'banquet' cuisine after the elaborate dishes which are popular at the Chinese-style banquets given in north Vietnam. Of all Vietnamese food, this style is the least suitable for cooking at home – it takes a long time to prepare and uses many different ingredients.

Hue in the centre of the country was the ancient capital of Vietnam. Beautiful presentation is a feature of the cuisine of the centre and small portions of many different dishes are served together at one meal. The food is hot and spicy with the constant use of chillies and shrimp sauce – the spices are said to ward off illnesses such as malaria and cholera. The highlands of the central region and the temperate climate provide Western-type vegetables such as asparagus, potatoes, cauliflower and artichokes.

Southern Vietnam is hot and humid. The tropical climate and fertile land provide a wealth of exotic fruits and vegetables and the Mekong river and its delta provide fish, together with vegetable crops and paddy fields for the rice. The cuisine of the south is more simple than that of the centre and north and the southern Vietnamese have a more relaxed, informal approach to cooking. Ingredients are of good quality and in plentiful supply, therefore they are allowed to speak for themselves in dishes rather than being mixed with many other ingredients. This makes for a fresher style of cooking which concentrates on the individual flavours of fish, fruits and vegetables. Certain ingredients are reserved for certain foods, rather than using the same mixture of spices for many different dishes as is the practice in the north, and many fruits and vegetables are eaten raw or only very lightly and quickly cooked so that the diner can fully appreciate the natural flavours, colours and textures of the food itself. Raw salads with fresh herbs feature prominently in the southern cuisine and food is cooked quickly by shallow-frying rather than deep-frying or stewing in oil. The custom of eating raw food arose out of the influence of the French and today most Vietnamese prefer to cook beef rare or at the most medium rare following the French tradition. The French influence can also be seen in the cooking techniques used in the south. Wine is used in certain dishes (the Vietnamese are Buddhists and therefore without restrictions on their diet) and stewing and casseroling are popular cooking methods for meat. Curries in the south are very, very hot, made with dried spices according to the Indian tradition. Coconut is used a great deal, sometimes with the addition of marijuana leaves for extra flavour.

Vietnamese meal patterns

The Vietnamese day begins bright and early at around 5 am for most people, in town and country alike. This is the coolest part of the day to start work, but the main reason for such early rising is that it is impossible to sleep through the noise! Accommodation is very crowded by Western standards, and the rickshaws, animals and chickens kick up a cacophonous din at dawn. Work begins at 7 am and breakfast is very often eaten walking along the street to work or school. Traditionally, breakfast is a very important meal in Vietnam, and rice noodle soup is the usual breakfast for everyone – or glutinous rice for those living in country districts. The Vietnamese have been heavily influenced by the French in their breakfast eating habits, however, and nowadays a croissant and a bowl of coffee are also popular, or a 'French bread' sandwich of cheese, roast chicken or ham.

Lunch is taken between 12 noon and 2 pm, when everything closes down for 'siesta'. Husbands and children come home for lunch, which is another important meal in the day. A bowl of 'potage' is generally served at lunchtime. This is a clear soup flavoured with either meat or shrimp which has fresh vegetables floating in it. The midday sun is so hot that the potage helps cool down the body; it also helps to push down the rice which is served at every meal. Other dishes served at lunchtime might be a mixture of stir-fried vegetables and a seafood dish such as grilled prawns or fried beef with bamboo shoot. For eighty per cent of the population all these dishes are placed on the table together and everyone helps themselves, drinking the potage throughout the meal.

Dinner in the evening between 5 and 6 pm is a similar meal to lunch, although probably more substantial. Dinner usually includes a bowl of rice, a dish of meat such as chicken, duck or pork, a fish dish, a vegetable stir-fry and a bowl of soup. The selection of dishes at one meal will have different flavours, varying from mild to very salty to achieve a balanced whole. Desserts are very rare and most evening meals finish simply with fresh fruit such as water melons, mangoes, durians, logans, lychees, jack fruit, star fruit and oranges. Cakes and sweets are not eaten after meals but as snacks

Above: Planting rice seedlings in North Vietnam

bought from street vendors during the day or offered to visitors when they call.

How food is served and eaten

In most Vietnamese homes, meals are taken around a low table called a *divan*, which is made of wood, about the same height as a Western coffee table. Men sit cross-legged around the table, women sit with their legs tucked in to one side. The table is laid with a simple straw mat, then each person has his or her own Chinese-style bowl and a set of wooden or lacquer chopsticks placed to the right of the bowl. A bottle of nuoc mam or a dip of nuoc cham is usually set on the table, in much the same way as tomato ketchup is seen at family meals in the West.

Food is brought to the table in large bowls by the women, the bowl of rice being placed next to the lady of the house who will serve everyone with a small portion. Everyone helps themselves to a little of one of the other dishes which is eaten on its own with the rice before another helping of rice is taken. Soup is drunk throughout the meal when it has cooled to tepid, either straight from the bowl or with a metal spoon. Chopsticks are used for every kind of food, never the fingers. Food is cut up small during preparation so that chopsticks are always adequate utensils.

Cooking equipment

There is very little special equipment needed for Vietnamese cooking. Good-quality sharp knives are obviously important as all ingredients are sliced or chopped during preparation so that food can be eaten easily with chopsticks at the table. A large cook's knife and a cleaver for chopping through bones are two of the most essential items.

Most Vietnamese food is either steamed or boiled in an ordinary large saucepan. For stir-frying, many Vietnamese use an ordinary heavy frying pan, but a deep, Chinese-style wok facilitates tossing and stirring large quantities of ingredients together, plus a pair of long 'master' chopsticks which should be kept in the kitchen especially for cooking purposes.

Various cooking fuels are used in Vietnam. Wood and coal fires are the traditional methods used for cooking, but in the cities bottled gas and kerosene can be found in many modern homes.

For pounding spices, fish and shrimps, a mortar and pestle is traditional, although an electric blender or food processor may be used if you prefer. The traditional Vietnamese mortar is made of stone, but it is an interesting fact that since the Vietnam war steel American helmets have become widely used. They are much stronger than the traditional stone mortar and therefore less likely to break.

Special Ingredients

Agar-Agar (thach) is a natural setting agent made from seaweed. It is used in the making of desserts. At health food shops and oriental stores it is available in long white strands or as a powder. Non-vegetarians may use gelatine as a substitute, but a small amount of agar-agar sets a larger volume of liquid than gelatine, so care must be taken over the quantity used.

Banana Essence (dau choi) is a bottled commercial flavouring. It is widely available at supermarkets. Bananas are native to Vietnam and widely used in both sweet and savoury dishes. Banana essence is used to intensify their flavour in sweet dishes.

Barbecue Sauce (tuong-den) is a commercially pre-pared bottled sauce, the same kind that is used in Chinese cooking. It is reddish in colour, sweet and salty in flavour. The Vietnamese use barbecue sauce mainly as a dip to serve with barbecued and grilled foods.

Bean Curd, Red Fermented (chao-do) should not be confused with the fresh white bean curd so widely used in oriental cooking. Red fermented bean curd is fla-voured and coloured with tomatoes and is sold in cans in oriental stores. It is more pungent than fresh bean curd, with a flavour like strong cheese. It is so strong in fact that it is never eaten on its own but is used in marinades for game birds and chicken (never for beef or pork) which are to be grilled or barbecued. A few small cubes are crushed with spices and soy sauce to make the marinade, which is very pungent.

Black Jack (nuoc mau) is a dark brown liquid colouring agent which is used in hotpots and stews, especially those made with beef and pork, to give a good, rich colour. It is not easy to obtain, but it can be made at home (see Note, page 24). Alternatively, use dark soy sauce.

Chinese Liqueur (mai kwai lo) is used in marinades for meat before barbecuing and grilling. It takes away impurities and blood, but it is not an essential ingre-dient. Rice alcohol can be used as a substitute.

Chinese mushrooms, dried (nam dong co) have a unique fragrant flavour and should not be confused with continental dried mushrooms, which are quite dif-ferent. Chinese dried mushrooms are available in packets at oriental stores, often called *shiitake*, which is their Japanese name. Although expensive, their strong flavour makes it possible to use them in small quan-tities. They should always be soaked in warm water before use, for about 30 minutes, then their tough stems should be cut off and discarded.

Chinese sausages (lap suong) are long and thin, made from pork. They are dried and should be steamed before use, then thinly sliced.

Chinese White Carrots, see White Radishes.

Curry Leaves (la cari) are available fresh and dried (the

curry leaf plant is very easy to grow in the garden and can be bought at most nurseries which stock a good selection of herbs). They are used by the Vietnamese in curries and also in beef stews. If only 1 or 2 leaves are used they impart a pleasant aromatic flavour — it is only when they are used in larger quantities than this that they give a 'curried' flavour.

Curry Powder is used in Vietnamese curries, but never Indian curry powder which the Vietnamese find too strong. Malaysian and Thai curry powders which can be bought in stores specialising in these foods are the types most favoured by the Vietnamese. They are mildly aromatic rather than being pungent and spicy.

1) Egg noodles; 2) Rice vermicelli; 3) Chinese white cabbage (bok choy); 4) Crab; 5) White radish; 6) Limes; 7) Star fruit; 8) Rhizome; 9) Chinese sausage; 10) Langoustines (crayfish); 11) Lemon grass; 12) Chinese mushrooms; 13) Bamboo shoots; 14) King prawn; 15) Red fermented bean curd; 16) Wood ear; 17) Curry leaves; 18) Shallots; 19) Palm sugar

8

9
.

Fish Sauce (nuoc mam) is the most pungent of all the fish sauces used in south-east Asian cooking. It is made from salted anchovies, sardines and other small fish which are layered with salt and dried in barrels in the sun. The resulting liquid is thin and salty with a very strong fish flavour. The Vietnamese use *nuoc mam* in cooking to bring out the flavour of other ingredients, they also use it as a condiment at the table in much the same way as the Chinese use soy sauce. The dip called *nuoc cham* is made from fish sauce mixed with garlic, chillies, sugar and lime or lemon.

Five Spice Powder (ngu vi huong) is an aromatic seasoning which is reddish-brown in colour. It is used all over south-east Asia, but particularly in China. The five spices are star anise, cloves, cinnamon, fennel and szechuan pepper. It should always be used sparingly as it has a strong flavour.

Jack Fruit (mit) is a tropical yellow fruit with a thick spiky skin. It should be peeled before use, then halved and stoned. The flesh is very sweet with a unique flavour and the fruit is eaten as a dessert on its own or mixed with other exotic fruit.

Lemon Grass (xa) is an aromatic plant which is widely available fresh in large supermarkets as well as oriental stores. It is used extensively in oriental cooking for its strong lemon fragrance and flavour. It is sold as stems with the bulbous root end attached. The root should be chopped, crushed or sliced and added to spice mixtures in the same way as fresh root ginger. The stem end is usually left whole and used in cooking for its flavour – it is removed before serving. If fresh lemon grass is unobtainable, dried lemon grass called *serai* can be bought in powder form. As a general guide, 1 tsp serai is equivalent to 1 stem of fresh lemon grass.

Longans (long nhan) are a succulent tree fruit from the same family as the lychee. Fresh longans have a smooth, yellow skin which must be peeled before eating. The flavour of longans is less pronounced than that of lychees, which may be substituted if preferred.

Maggi Sauce is a liquid seasoning sold in bottles in supermarkets as well as oriental stores. Although a western condiment, it is used extensively in oriental cooking to bring out the flavour of other ingredients.

Oyster Sauce (dau hao) is a commercially prepared bottled sauce made from oysters and soy sauce. It is thick and brown, used to add extra flavour in cooking, especially in Chinese-style dishes. It is mostly used in stir-fries, fried noodle dishes and with blanched vegetables.

Palm Sugar (duong the) is also known as *jaggery* or *gula Malacca*. It is made from the sap of palm trees, which is boiled until it crystallizes then formed into flat, round cakes. To use palm sugar in sweet dishes it must first be grated, shredded or chopped. If unobtainable, use unrefined dark brown barbados sugar instead.

Pickled Bamboo Shoots (mang chua) are sold sliced in jars. They are marinated in vinegar and spices and so taste very sour and hot. Before use they should be soaked in water to remove some of the sourness. The Vietnamese use them mostly in stocks, soups and gravies, and they are especially popular with duck.

Pickled Vegetables (dua chua) are used as a garnish or trimming for *nem* (Vietnamese pancakes). In Vietnam, cooks shred and pickle their own vegetables, but this is time-consuming and only practical if you are eating Vietnamese food regularly. A quick substitute for homemade pickled vegetables is to shred bottled pickled gherkins and onions and combine them with very finely shredded cabbage and carrot, including some of the liquid from the gherkins and onions.

Plum Sauce (cuong ngot) is a commercially bottled sauce used in Chinese-style dishes for its sweet and spicy flavour. It is made from a combination of plums, sugar, chillies, spices and vinegar and should be used with caution as some brands can be quite hot.

Rhizome (cu gieng) is a root rather like ginger. It is used in savoury dishes, most often with stewed fish. It is available at specialist oriental shops, but fresh root ginger can be used as a substitute. The two are dealt with in exactly the same way.

Rice Alcohol (ruou de) is made from fermented steamed white rice. It is used both as an ingredient in cooking and as a drink. If serving it as a drink it should be warm – simply immerse the bottle in very hot water to heat it up. In cooking, dry sherry may be used as a substitute.

Rice Noodles (banh pho) are very thick, wide and flat like Italian pasta. They can be bought fresh at oriental stores as well as dried. Fresh rice noodles are used for stir-fry dishes, dried are used in soups.

Rice Papers (banh trang) are thin, brittle dried wrappers used for making *nem* (Vietnamese pancakes) and *Cha gio* (spring rolls). Before use they should be dipped in water to soften them so that they become pliable.

Rice Vermicelli (bun) are transparent or cellophane noodles made from mung bean flour. Sold dried, they are very fine, almost like string, and are used in many savoury dishes, especially soups and as a garnish for *nem* (Vietnamese pancakes) and *cha gio* (spring rolls). If they are to be fried, they should first be soaked in water for about 10 minutes, then drained before use.

Salted Black Beans (tuong hot den) are available in cans and jars. They are soya beans which have been steamed, spiced and heavily salted. They are used in Chinese-style dishes for their salty flavour – and nutritional value. When they are used in long-cooking dishes such as stews and hotpots they are left whole, but for quick-cooking stir-fries they must first be crushed, which will also help release their flavour.

Shallots, Dried (hanh huong) are sold in packets in oriental stores. In Vietnamese cooking they are very finely sliced and deep-fried until crisp and golden brown, then sprinkled on top of certain savoury dishes as a garnish. Fresh shallots can be used if dried are difficult to obtain, but the flavour and texture will not be quite the same.

Star Anise (hoi) is the dried fruit of a Chinese tree. It is a pretty star shape, hence its name. The Vietnamese use it in Chinese-style dishes.

Star Fruit (khe), also called *carambolas*, are a long waxy fruit which have five ribs. When they are cut across, the slices are star-shaped. The Vietnamese use unripe green star fruit to add sourness and acidity to pickled vegetables (see above). Ripe, yellow star fruit are eaten as a dessert fruit. They are available at most large supermarkets and specialist greengrocers and markets.

Tangerine Peel, Dried (vo quit) is used in Chinese-style dishes for its strong, piquant flavour. It is available in Chinese specialist shops, but if you are unable to obtain it you may substitute the fresh peel of tangerines, mandarins or oranges. Dried tangerine peel is very concentrated in flavour, therefore you have to use at least twice as much fresh to obtain a similar strength.

White Radishes (cu cai trang) are also known as Japanese radishes, *mooli* and *daikon*. They are used extensively in oriental cooking, both as a garnish and a cooked vegetable. Long, thin and white, they have a crisp texture and a unique nutty flavour.

Wood Ears (moc nhi) are a dried black fungus also sometimes sold under the name 'cloud ears'. They get their name from their shape — when soaked in water they look like gelatinous ears. They have no flavour of their own, but are used for their texture and the fact that they very quickly absorb flavours from other ingredients in the same dish.

Menus

Lunch Party

Chicken and transparent rice vermicelli soup

Pacific prawns in tomato sauce, with pickled vegetables and boiled rice

Stir-fried beef with bamboo shoot

Sautéed Aubergine

Vegetarian Dinner

Vegetarian Spring Rolls

Sweet and Sour Chinese Mushrooms

Egg Soup, made with vegetable stock

Crispy Bean Curd with Tomato Sauce

Fried Rice with Egg

Buffet Party

Crispy Spring Rolls with Anchovy Sauce

Prawn Toasts

Pork and Lettuce Parcels

Prawns in Batter

Meduse Salad

Fruit Salad Ice Mountain

Dinner Party

Prawn Balls with Accompaniments (see recipe)

Duck, Bamboo Shoot and Rice Vermicelli Soup

Grilled Red Mullet

Grilled Skewers of Chicken with Five Spices

Caramel Pork

Asparagus with Crabmeat

Plain Boiled Rice

Chilled Avocado with Condensed Milk

Barbecue

Grilled Langoustine

Hot and Spicy Quail

Grilled Beef in Vine Leaves

Barbecued Pork Spare Ribs with Lemon Grass

Vietnamese Green Salad

Plain Boiled Rice

Family Supper

Chicken and Mushroom Soup

Fried Crispy Noodles with Chicken, Ham and Prawns

Crabmeat Omelettes

Tomatoes Stuffed with Pork

11

Ṣnacks & Ṣoups

In this chapter you'll find a range of dishes suitable for many occasions. The snacks that open the chapter can be enjoyed at any time. They will also make excellent starters for a more elaborate Vietnamese meal, and provide an original element in a selection of party or buffet food. The soups that follow can also be enjoyed as starters in a Western-style three-course meal, or as main-course supper dishes in their own right.

Prawn Balls

Chao Tom

*500 g (1 lb) raw prawns, shelled and deveined
(see Transparent Spring Rolls, opposite)
2 teaspoons salt
50 g (2 oz) boiled fat pork, diced
1 small onion, finely chopped
4 cloves garlic, crushed
½ teaspoon baking powder
½ teaspoon white pepper
pinch of monosodium glutamate (optional)
oil for deep-frying*

*To serve:
lettuce leaves
fresh coriander leaves
barbecue sauce
plum sauce
ground roasted peanuts*

Prepare the prawn paste: place the prawns in a large bowl with the salt. Using clean hands scoop up the prawns, pressing and squeezing them to remove excess liquid. Transfer to a colander and rinse under cold water. Pat dry with paper towels or spread the mixture out and allow to dry naturally for 1 hour.

Spoon the prawns into a food processor or blender, add the fat pork and grind to a smooth paste. Scrape the paste into a bowl, add the remaining ingredients (except the oil) and mix well.

Taking about 1 heaped teaspoon of the prawn paste at a time, roll it between well-oiled hands to form small balls about the size of shallots. Set aside.

Heat the oil in a wok or deep-fat fryer and cook the balls, a few at a time, until golden brown. Remove with a slotted spoon and drain on paper towels. Serve with lettuce and coriander leaves and a selection of sauces, such as barbecue and plum sauce, sprinkled with roasted peanuts.

Note: If preferred, the prawn balls may be cooked under a preheated low grill for 4 to 5 minutes. Carefully turn the balls so that they cook on all sides.

Chicken Wings with Garlic Butter

Canh Ga Chien Bo

*16 chicken wings
5 tablespoons butter
4 cloves garlic, crushed
1 teaspoon Maggi seasoning*

Prepare the chicken by breaking each wing in half along the joint, working the bones loose with your fingers and then turning the wings inside out to remove the bones.

Melt 4 tablespoons of the butter in a frying pan, add the chicken and shallow-fry over moderate heat for 8 to 10 minutes or until cooked. Remove the chicken with a slotted spoon and reserve.

Add the remaining butter to the pan. When it sizzles, stir in the garlic and fry for 3 to 4 minutes until golden brown. Stir in the Maggi seasoning, return the chicken to the pan and toss over high heat for 1 minute to heat through. Serve immediately.

Left: Transparent Spring Rolls; right: Prawn Balls

13

Transparent Spring Rolls

Goi Cuon

225 g (8 oz) pork fillet
50 g (2 oz) transparent rice vermicelli
100 g (4 oz) prawns, shelled, deveined and
cut in half lengthways (see Note) then cooked
50 g (2 oz) bean sprouts
12 sheets banh trang (rice paper)
1 small round lettuce, shredded
2 tablespoons shredded fresh mint leaves
3 tablespoons ground roasted peanuts
nuoc mam giam
(see Crispy Spring Rolls, page 14) to serve

These spring rolls differ from their crispy counterparts (recipe on page 14) because the wrappers are uncooked and transparent, allowing the filling to be seen.

Place the pork in a saucepan with water or vegetable stock to cover. Bring to the boil, lower the heat and simmer for 15 to 20 minutes or until the pork is cooked. Set aside and, when cold, cut into thin strips.

Bring a large saucepan of water to the boil, add the vermicelli and cook for 2 to 3 minutes or until tender. Drain in a colander, rinse well under cold water, then drain again. Place in a large bowl with the pork, prawns and bean sprouts. Mix gently.

Dip the sheets of banh trang in cold water, carefully shake off excess water, and lay the sheets on a clean work surface. Divide the filling between them, piling it along one end of each sheet, about 2.5 cm (1 inch) from the end and a similar distance from the sides.

Add shredded lettuce, mint leaves and peanuts to each filling, turn in the sides and roll up the banh trang, sausage-fashion. Arrange on a large platter and serve with nuoc mam giam sauce.

Note: To prepare uncooked prawns, start by removing the heads — they should pull away fairly easily. Peel off the skins, working from the head end to the tail, then remove the sharp, central rib of the tail, leaving the side pieces.

With a sharp knife, cut each prawn along the centre, stopping short of its tail. Open out and remove the central vein. Cook as usual.

Prawn Toasts

Banh Mi Chien Tom

Prawn paste (see Prawn Balls)
6 slices white bread, crusts removed
oil for deep-frying

Prepare the prawn paste as in the previous recipe, but do not roll it into balls. Instead, spread it evenly on each slice of bread, almost, but not quite, to the edges. Use the blade of the knife to press the mixture firmly on to the bread.

Heat the oil in a wok or deep-fat fryer. Using a fish slice, slide a piece of prawn-covered bread into the oil. When the edges of the bread turn golden, carefully turn the toast over. Fry until golden brown. Remove, drain on paper towels and keep hot. Repeat until all the slices of toast are cooked, then cut the toasts into neat fingers or squares and serve immediately.

Crispy Spring Rolls

Cha Gio

50 g (2 oz) transparent rice vermicelli
15 g (½ oz) wood ears (dry weight)
25 g (1 oz) dried Chinese mushrooms
150 g (5 oz) minced pork
100 g (4 oz) drained canned water chestnuts,
finely chopped
1 medium carrot, finely chopped
100 g (4 oz) crabmeat, picked over and flaked
1 onion, finely chopped
3 teaspoons salt
½ teaspoon finely ground black pepper
1 egg
12 sheets banh trang (rice paper)
water or beaten egg to seal
oil for deep-frying

Nuoc mam giam sauce:
1 clove garlic, roughly chopped
1 fresh red chilli, roughly chopped
1 tablespoon nuoc mam (fish gravy)
1 teaspoon lemon juice or vinegar
1 tablespoon tepid water
1 tablespoon sugar

To serve:
1 lettuce, separated into leaves
2 sprigs fresh mint leaves

These delicious spring rolls are served with a sauce which is as vital to Vietnamese cooking as salt is in the West. Its basis, nuoc mam, is an essential store-cupboard staple for anyone wishing to cook Vietnamese food.

Place the vermicelli in a large bowl, add warm water to cover and set aside for 15 minutes. Combine the wood ears and dried mushrooms in a small bowl, cover with warm water and set aside for 15 minutes. When both vermicelli and mushrooms are soft, drain thoroughly and chop finely. Place in a large bowl.

Stir in the minced pork, chopped water chestnuts, carrot, crabmeat and onion. Mix thoroughly with a wooden spoon.

Add the salt, pepper and egg and mix well, using clean hands to press and mould the mixture together. Divide the mixture into 12 equal-sized portions and roll each to a sausage shape.

Dip the sheets of banh trang in cold water, shake off any excess water, and lay the banh trang on a clean work surface. Place one of the stuffing 'sausages' on one end of a single sheet of banh trang, turn in the sides to enclose the filling and roll up, sealing the ends with a little water or beaten egg.

Repeat this process to make 12 spring rolls in all. Place in the refrigerator to chill while preparing the sauce.

To make the nuoc mam giam sauce, grind the garlic and chilli together in a blender or food processor, or pound in a mortar with a pestle. Transfer to a small bowl, stir in the remaining ingredients and mix well.

Heat the oil in a wok or deep-fat fryer. Add the rolls, a few at a time, and deep-fry until golden brown. Drain on paper towels and serve immediately, with lettuce, mint leaves and the prepared dipping sauce.

Crabmeat and Asparagus Soup

Sup Cua Mang Tay

1.5 litres (2½ pints) chicken stock
1 teaspoon salt
freshly ground black pepper
pinch of monosodium glutamate (optional)
300 g (11 oz) crabmeat, picked over and flaked
1 x 340 g (12 oz) can asparagus spears, drained and
cut into 2.5 cm (1 inch) lengths
1 tablespoon cornflour
4 tablespoons water
1 egg white, lightly beaten

Bring the stock to the boil in a large saucepan and season with salt, pepper and monosodium glutamate, if using. Stir in the crabmeat and asparagus.

Combine the cornflour and water in a cup and mix to a cream. Add to the soup and cook, stirring gently with a wooden spoon, until it thickens. Allow the mixture to boil for 2 minutes more, stirring occasionally.

Stirring constantly, add the egg white, which will form threads. Serve immediately, with more pepper, if liked.

Left: Prawn Toasts; right: Crispy Spring Rolls

Egg Soup

Sup Trung

25 g (1 oz) dried Chinese mushrooms
1 litre (1¾ pints) chicken stock
1 x 340 g (12 oz) can asparagus tips, drained
1 teaspoon salt
pinch of monosodium glutamate (optional)
3 eggs, beaten
1 teaspoon sesame oil
200 g (7 oz) fresh watercress, washed
freshly ground black pepper

Place the mushrooms in a small bowl with warm water to cover. Soak for 15 minutes, then drain thoroughly and slice thinly.

Bring the stock to the boil in a large saucepan. Add the asparagus and mushrooms and cook for 2 minutes, then season with salt and monosodium glutamate, if using.

Add the beaten eggs, stirring the soup gently. Cook for 1 minute more. Stir in the sesame oil.

Just before serving arrange a portion of watercress in each of 4 bowls. Top each bowl with soup, sprinkle with pepper and and serve immediately.

Chicken Soup with Mushrooms

Sup Nam Ga

1 litre (1¾ pints) chicken stock
2 cooked chicken breasts, shredded
200 g (7 oz) drained canned straw mushrooms
1 x 340 g (11 oz) can asparagus tips, drained and halved lengthways
salt
2–3 tablespoons nuoc mam (fish gravy)
pinch of monosodium glutamate (optional)

Bring the stock to the boil in a large saucepan. Add the chicken, mushrooms and asparagus and season with salt, nuoc mam and monosodium glutamate, if using.

Lower the heat and simmer the soup for 5 minutes. Test the seasoning and add more salt or nuoc mam if necessary. Serve immediately.

Chicken and Transparent Rice Vermicelli Soup

Mien Ga

10 pieces wood ear
100 g (4 oz) transparent rice vermicelli
1 × 1.5 kg (3 lb) chicken
3 tablespoons nuoc mam (fish gravy)
1 teaspoon salt
½ teaspoon monosodium glutamate (optional)

To serve:
2 spring onions, finely sliced
2 tablespoons chopped fresh coriander
freshly ground black pepper

Place the wood ears in a small bowl with warm water to cover. Soak for 10 minutes, then drain, chop finely and reserve.

Bring a large saucepan of water to the boil, add the vermicelli, lower the heat and simmer for 3 to 5 minutes. Drain in a colander, rinse well under cold water, then drain again. Set aside, in the colander, until required.

Place the chicken in a large deep saucepan, add water to about 7.5 cm (3 inches) above the chicken, and bring to the boil. Lower the heat and simmer for about 1½ to 2 hours or until the chicken is tender. Remove the chicken from the stock and set it aside. Reserve the stock. When cool, discard the skin from the chicken and shred the flesh.

Blot the chicken stock with paper towels to remove excess fat. (Alternatively, allow the stock to cool and leave in the refrigerator overnight, when the fat will have separated and be easy to remove.) Season with nuoc mam, salt and monosodium glutamate (if using). Add the chopped wood ears and simmer the stock for 5 minutes more.

Just before serving, pour boiling water through the vermicelli in the colander to warm it. Divide between 4 soup bowls, adding a little shredded chicken to each. Top up with stock and serve immediately, sprinkled with sliced spring onions, coriander and pepper.

Hot and Sour Fish Soup

Canh Chua Ca

225 g (8 oz) cod fillets
2 litres (3½ pints) water
4 tablespoons lemon juice
2 tomatoes, quartered and seeded
1–2 fresh red chillies, finely chopped
3 tablespoons nuoc mam (fish gravy)
1 teaspoon salt
pinch of monosodium glutamate (optional)
1 small bunch dill leaves, finely chopped, to serve

Place the fish in a large saucepan with the water and bring to the boil. Lower the heat and simmer for 12 to 15 minutes or until the fish is cooked (the flesh should flake easily when tested with a fork).

Remove the pan from the heat and add the lemon juice, tomatoes and chillies. Season with the nuoc mam, salt and monosodium glutamate (if using). Pour the soup into a large heated bowl or tureen and serve immediately, sprinkled with chopped dill leaves.
Note: For a more substantial soup, add rice vermicelli as Duck, Bamboo Shoot and Rice Vermicelli Soup.

Beef and Rice Noodle Soup

Pho

1 piece (about 2.5 cm/1 inch) root ginger
1 small onion
50 g (2 oz) rice noodles
1 kg (2 lb) beef shin or brisket
1½ tablespoons salt
2 litres (3½ pints) water
1 herb sachet comprising 5 cloves, 3 star anise and 10 coriander seeds
100 g (4 oz) fillet steak, cut into very thin slices

To serve:
2 tablespoons chopped spring onions
2 tablespoons chopped fresh coriander leaves
4–6 teaspoons nuoc mam (fish gravy)

This dish is a North Vietnamese speciality, often served as a snack food in restaurants.

Place the ginger under a preheated moderately hot grill for about 15 minutes or until the skin blackens. Set aside until cool, then scrape off the blackened skin, grate the flesh and reserve. Prepare the unpeeled onion in the same way, grilling until the skin blackens and the centre is soft. When cool, peel the onion and chop the flesh. Set aside.

Bring a large saucepan of water to the boil, add the noodles and cook for 3 to 5 minutes or until tender. Drain in a colander, rinse well under cold water, then drain again. Set aside, in the colander, until required.

Place the beef in a large saucepan with the salt. Add water to cover. Bring to the boil and cook vigorously for 2 minutes, then drain. Rinse well under cold water, drain again and return to the cleaned saucepan. Add the measured water and bring to the boil. Lower the heat and simmer for 1½ hours, uncovered, until the water is reduced by one third.

Add the herb sachet, ginger and onion and simmer the beef for 1 hour more. Strain. (The beef will have lost all of its flavour by now and can be discarded.)

Just before serving, pour boiling water through the noodles in the colander to warm them. Divide between 4 soup bowls and top each portion with raw fillet steak. Fill each bowl with the beef stock, sprinkle with chopped spring onions and coriander leaves and serve immediately, with a bowl of nuoc mam. Each guest adds a little nuoc mam to his or her soup – about 1 teaspoon is usually enough. If the taste is too dominant, squeeze in a little fresh lemon juice. The hot broth will warm the fillet steak through, cooking it very rarely.

Pork, Shrimp and Rice Noodle Soup

Hu Tieu

25 g (1 oz) dried shrimps
50 g (2 oz) rice noodles
225 g (8 oz) pork spare ribs or hand, sliced
2 litres (3½ pints) water
3 tablespoons nuoc mam (fish gravy)
½ teaspoon salt

To serve:
2 tablespoons chopped spring onions
2 tablespoons chopped fresh coriander leaves
sesame oil

Soak the dried shrimps in a small bowl with warm water to cover for 15 minutes. Drain and set aside.

Bring a large saucepan of water to the boil, add the noodles and cook for 3 to 5 minutes or until just tender. Drain in a colander, rinse well under cold water, then drain again. Set aside, in the colander, until required.

Place the shrimps and pork in a large saucepan with the measured water. Bring to the boil, lower the heat and simmer for 1½ hours, until the stock is reduced by one third.

Strain and stir in the nuoc mam and salt.

Just before serving, pour boiling water through the noodles in the colander to warm them. Divide between 4 soup bowls. Add 2 to 3 slices of cooked pork to each bowl and top up with the reduced shrimp and pork stock. Sprinkle with chopped spring onions, chopped fresh coriander leaves and a few drops of sesame oil. Serve immediately.

Left: Pork, Shrimp and Rice Noodle Soup; right: Beef and Rice Noodle Soup

Duck, Bamboo Shoot and Rice Vermicelli Soup

Bun Sao Vit

100 g (4 oz) pickled bamboo shoot
100 g (4 oz) rice vermicelli
1 × 1.75 kg (4 lb) duck
1 iceberg lettuce, cut into small cubes
½ cucumber, shredded
2 tablespoons fresh coriander leaves
2 tablespoons fresh mint leaves
3 tablespoons nuoc mam (fish gravy)
1 teaspoon salt
freshly ground black pepper to taste

Pickled bamboo shoot has a strong, rather sour taste that could overwhelm the flavour of the duck in this soup. To lessen its sharpness, soak the bamboo shoot in warm water to cover for 20 minutes before use, then drain and reserve.

Bring a large saucepan of water to the boil, add the vermicelli, lower the heat and simmer for 3 to 5 minutes. Drain in a colander, rinse well under cold water, then drain again. Set aside until required.

Place the duck in a large deep saucepan, add water to about 7.5 cm (3 inches) above the duck and bring slowly to the boil. Lower the heat and simmer very gently for 1 to 1½ hours or until the duck is tender. Remove the duck from the stock and set it aside to drain well. Reserve the stock, placing it in the refrigerator overnight if time allows.

When cool, discard the skin from the duck and chop the flesh into large chunks. Arrange these on a large platter with the lettuce, cucumber, coriander and mint leaves.

Skim the duck stock or blot it with paper towels to remove excess fat. (If you have had time to leave it in the refrigerator overnight, the fat will have separated and solidified and can be removed easily.) Add the prepared pickled bamboo shoot with the nuoc mam, salt and pepper. Mix well and simmer for 15 minutes more.

Just before serving, pour boiling water through the vermicelli in the colander to warm it. Divide between 4 soup bowls, topping each bowl with the duck stock. Serve the soup with the platter of duck meat and vegetables, so that guests can flavour the soup to their own taste.

Left: Duck, Bamboo Shoot and Rice Vermicelli Soup; right: Chicken and Rice Soup

Chicken and Rice Soup

Chao Ga

1 × 1.5 kg (3 lb) chicken
100 g (4 oz) long-grain rice, pre-cooked
1 teaspoon nuoc mam (fish gravy)
1 teaspoon salt
pinch of monosodium glutamate (optional)

To serve:
4 spring onions, blanched
white pepper

Place the chicken in a large deep saucepan, add water to about 7.5 cm (3 inches) above the chicken and bring to the boil. Lower the heat and simmer for about 1½ to 2 hours or until the chicken is tender. Remove the chicken from the stock and set it aside. When cool, discard the skin, shred the chicken flesh and reserve. Allow the stock to cool slightly.

Blot the chicken stock with paper towels to remove excess fat. (Alternatively, allow the stock to cool and leave in the refrigerator overnight, when the fat will have separated and be easy to remove.) Return the saucepan to the heat and allow the stock to return to the boil. Add the rice, lower the heat slightly and cook until it is soft, about 20 minutes – the grains should open out.

Season the rice soup with the nuoc mam, salt and monosodium glutamate (if using). Return the shredded chicken to the pan and stir well. Simmer for 5 minutes.

Pour the soup into a large heated bowl or tureen, add the spring onions, sprinkle with white pepper and serve immediately.

Duck and Rice Soup

Chao Vit

1 × 1.75 kg (4 lb) duck
100 g (4 oz) long-grain rice, pre-cooked
1 teaspoon nuoc mam (fish gravy) or to taste
1 teaspoon salt
pinch of monosodium glutamate (optional)
2 tablespoons finely chopped spring onions

Gingery nuoc mam giam sauce:
2–3 slices root ginger, peeled
2 fresh red chillies, roughly chopped
1 tablespoon lemon juice or vinegar
1 tablespoon nuoc mam (fish gravy)
5 teaspoons sugar or to taste
1 tablespoon warm water

Place the duck in a large deep saucepan, add water to about 7.5 cm (3 inches) above the duck and bring to the boil. Lower the heat and simmer for 1 to 1½ hours or until the duck is tender. Remove the duck from the stock and set it aside. Reserve the stock.

When the duck is cool, discard the skin and carve the flesh into large slices. Arrange on a platter and set aside.

Skim the duck stock or blot it with paper towels to remove excess fat. (Alternatively, allow the stock to cool and leave in the refrigerator overnight, when the fat will have separated and be easy to remove.) Return the saucepan to the heat and allow the stock to return to the boil. Add the rice, lower the heat slightly and cook until it is soft, about 15 minutes.

Meanwhile, prepare the gingery nuoc mam giam. Grind the ginger and chillies together in a blender or food processor, or pound in a mortar with a pestle. Transfer to a small bowl, stir in the remaining ingredients and mix well.

Season the rice soup with the nuoc mam, salt and monosodium glutamate (if using). Stir well and simmer for 5 minutes.

Pour the soup into 4 individual soup bowls, top each with finely chopped spring onions and serve immediately. The pieces of duck are served separately and are dipped in the gingery nuoc mam giam sauce before being eaten.

Fish & Shellfish

Vietnam enjoys the benefit of a coastline from top to bottom of the country, and the influence of the sea on its cooking is enormous. Many of Vietnam's finest dishes make use of fish of various sorts, often in original ways: the Stuffed Squid on page 22 is a feast of texture as much as taste, while the Fish au Caramel on page 24 demonstrates the effectiveness of an unusual flavour combination. Large seafood is a speciality of the South China Sea, and you'll also find recipes using langoustine, eel, sea bass and sea bream.

Prawns in Batter

Tom Chieu Bot

24 Pacific prawns, shelled and deveined (see Transparent Spring Rolls, page 13)
oil for deep-frying

Batter:
1 egg white
40 g (1½ oz) self-raising flour
1 level tablespoon plain flour
pinch of salt
pinch of monosodium glutamate (optional)
2 teaspoons vegetable oil
350 ml (12 fl oz) water

To serve:
120 ml (4 fl oz) lemon juice or sweet and sour sauce

Pat the prawns dry with paper towels. Open each prawn out a little to resemble a butterfly. Set aside.

Place the egg white in a bowl and beat until stiff.

In a mixing bowl, beat the flours, salt, monosodium glutamate (if using), vegetable oil and water to a smooth paste. Fold in the egg white and set the batter aside for 30 minutes.

Heat the oil in a deep-fat fryer. Holding a prawn by the tip of the tail, dip it in batter and gently drop it into the hot oil, taking care not to allow the hot fat to spatter. Add several more battered prawns to the pan and cook until puffed and golden. Deep-fry the remainder of the prawns in batches.

Drain the cooked prawns on paper towels and serve immediately, with a dip of lemon juice or sweet and sour sauce.

Variation: Shelled crab claws may be substituted for Pacific prawns, if preferred.

Spicy Pacific Prawns

Tom Xao Cay

5 tablespoons vegetable oil
2 cloves garlic, crushed
½ onion, finely chopped
500 g (1 lb) raw Pacific prawns, shelled and deveined (see Transparent Spring Rolls, page 13)
2 tablespoons nuoc mam (fish gravy)
½ teaspoon white pepper
12 peppercorns, lightly crushed
pinch of monosodium glutamate (optional)
1 teaspoon sugar
4 fresh green chillies, finely chopped
175 ml (6 fl oz) chicken stock

Heat the oil in a saucepan or wok, add the garlic and onion and stir-fry for 3 to 4 minutes until golden brown. Add the prawns and stir-fry for 1 minute.

Stir in the remaining ingredients and simmer, stirring occasionally, for 5 to 6 minutes or until the liquid has reduced and forms a thick sauce.

Serve immediately, with rice, if liked.

Left: Pacific Prawns in Tomato Sauce; right: Prawns in Batter

Pacific Prawns in Tomato Sauce

Tom Rang

500 g (1 lb) raw Pacific prawns, heads and legs removed, cleaned (see Transparent Spring Rolls, page 13)
4 tablespoons vegetable oil
2 cloves garlic, crushed
2 shallots, finely chopped
100 g (4 oz) drained canned tomatoes, or 3 fresh tomatoes, skinned, seeded and chopped
1 tablespoon soy sauce
pinch of salt
½ teaspoon sugar
1 tablespoon nuoc mam (fish gravy) or to taste
250 ml (8 fl oz) water
freshly ground black pepper

To serve:
pickled vegetables
boiled rice

Wash the prawns and pat dry on paper towels.

Heat the oil in a large frying pan, add half the garlic and shallots and fry for 3 to 4 minutes or until golden brown. Lower the heat, add the prawns and cook until pink, about 2 to 3 minutes. Remove the prawns with tongs or a slotted spoon and keep warm while making the sauce.

Add the remaining garlic and shallots to the oil remaining in the pan and fry for 2 to 3 minutes. Stir in the tomatoes, soy sauce, salt, sugar and nuoc mam. The flavour should be rich and salty.

Stir the water into the mixture, return the prawns to the pan and bring the liquid to the boil. Reduce the heat and simmer, stirring occasionally, for 3 to 4 minutes or until the liquid has reduced slightly and forms a thick sauce.

Transfer to a serving dish, sprinkle with pepper and garnish with pickled vegetables. Serve immediately, with rice.

Stuffed Squid

Muc Don Thit

12 medium squid, heads removed, cleaned
25 g (1 oz) transparent rice vermicelli
8 pieces of dried Chinese mushrooms
15 g (½ oz) wood ears (dry weight)
150 g (5 oz) minced pork
4 tablespoons finely chopped water chestnuts
1 clove garlic, crushed
½ onion, finely chopped
½ teaspoon salt
½ teaspoon freshly ground black pepper
½ teaspoon sugar
1 tablespoon nuoc mam (fish gravy)
1 egg, beaten
oil for deep-frying
nuoc mam giam (see Crispy Spring Rolls, page 14)

Prepare the squid: with clean hands dipped in salt, rub the skin off the body. Carefully remove the long internal quill-like bone, keeping the squid whole. Wash each squid thoroughly and pat dry with paper towels.

Place the vermicelli in a large bowl, add warm water to cover and set aside for 15 minutes. Place the dried mushrooms and wood ears in a second bowl and soak in warm water for 15 minutes. When both vermicelli and mushrooms are soft, drain thoroughly, chop finely and place in a large bowl.

Stir in the minced pork, chopped water chestnuts, garlic and onion. Add the salt, pepper, sugar and nuoc mam and mix well. Bind the stuffing with the egg.

Fill each squid with stuffing and close the neck cavities with bamboo skewers. Do not pack the squid too tightly.

Arrange the squid in the top of a steamer. Place over boiling water, cover and steam for 15 minutes. Allow the squid to cool.

Heat the oil in a deep-fat fryer or wok and deep-fry the stuffed squid, a few at a time, until golden brown.

To serve, slice the hot squid neatly and arrange on a platter, with nuoc mam giam as a dipping sauce.

Grilled Langoustines

Crab Claw and Prawn Paste Parcels

Cang Cua Boc Tom Bam

prawn paste (see Prawn Balls, page 12)
12 shelled crab claws, thawed and cooked
oil for deep-frying
barbecue or plum sauce to serve

Prepare the prawn paste. Roll each crab claw in the mixture, using oiled hands to press and mould the paste to a firm coating.

Heat the oil in a wok or deep-fat fryer and cook the crab claws, a few at a time, until golden brown. Remove with a slotted spoon and drain on paper towels.

Serve hot with barbecue or plum sauce.

Note: If preferred, the Crab Claw and Prawn Paste Parcels may be cooked under a preheated low grill for 4 to 5 minutes. Turn the claws over carefully halfway through cooking.

Grilled Langoustines

Tom Cang Nuong

oil for deep-frying
12 large langoustines, cleaned
225 g (8 oz) boiled fat pork, cut into 32 cubes
2 tablespoons chopped shallots
2 tablespoons chopped spring onion tops
24 sheets banh trang (rice paper)
1 iceburg lettuce, shredded
½ cucumber, thinly sliced
1 tablespoon fresh mint leaves
1 tablespoon chopped fresh coriander leaves
nuoc mam giam (see Crispy Spring Rolls, page 14)
to serve

Heat the oil in a wok or deep-fat fryer, add the langoustines and cook for 30 to 45 seconds. Remove the langoustines with a slotted spoon and drain on paper towels. Reduce the heat to low.

When the langoustines are cool enough to handle, shell and devein them (see Transparent Spring Rolls, page 13). Cut each langoustine in half lengthways.

Thread 3 langoustine halves and 4 pork cubes alternately on to 8 metal skewers, beginning and ending with pork.

Place the chopped shallots and spring onion tops in a small bowl. Using a soup ladle, scoop up a little of the hot oil in which the langoustines were cooked and add this to the bowl. Mix well.

Arrange the langoustine kebabs on a grid over medium to hot coals, or under a preheated medium grill, and brush liberally with the aromatic oil mixture. Cook for 5 to 8 minutes, turning frequently and brushing several times with the aromatic oil.

Meanwhile, prepare the banh trang by soaking them in tepid water for 1 minute. Shake off excess water, roll the banh trang loosely and arrange on a large platter with the lettuce, cucumber, mint and coriander leaves. Place the nuoc mam giam sauce in a bowl.

When the langoustines and pork cubes are cooked, slide them off the skewers on to a second platter and serve. Guests make their own rice paper rolls, using a half langoustine, one or two pork cubes and a selection of vegetables as the filling for each roll, and dipping the rolls in the nuoc mam giam sauce.

Steamed Eel

Loun Um

1 × 750 g (1½ lb) whole eel
175 ml (6 fl oz) rice alcohol or vodka
25 g (1 oz) transparent rice vermicelli
25 g (1 oz) wood ears (dry weight)
100 g (4 oz) minced pork
1 onion, finely chopped
3–4 fresh thyme leaves, finely chopped
salt
freshly ground black pepper
350 ml (12 fl oz) coconut cream (see Note)
2 tablespoons ground roasted peanuts to serve

Fillet the eel and clean the skin by rubbing it all over with rice alcohol or vodka. Set aside.

Place the vermicelli in a bowl, add warm water to cover and set aside for 15 minutes. Place the wood ears in a second bowl and soak in warm water for 15 minutes. When both vermicelli and wood ears are soft, drain thoroughly, chop finely and place in a large bowl.

Add the minced pork, onion and finely chopped thyme leaves. Mix thoroughly. Season with salt and pepper and use clean hands to press and mould the mixture into balls, about 5 cm (2 inches) in diameter.

Cut the filleted eel into slices large enough to enclose each meat ball. Wrap the balls in eel fillets and secure with string.

Arrange the eel 'parcels' in the top of one or two steamers, place over boiling water and steam for 30 minutes.

Meanwhile, simmer the coconut cream in a small saucepan until thick. Add salt and pepper to taste.

Arrange the steamed eel parcels on a heated platter, pour the coconut cream over and sprinkle with ground roasted peanuts. Serve immediately.

Note: To make the coconut cream, combine 400 g (14 oz) grated or desiccated coconut in a saucepan with 900 ml (1½ pints) milk. Simmer over low heat, stirring occasionally, until the mixture is reduced by one third. Strain, pressing the mixture against the sides of the strainer to extract as much liquid as possible, then pour the coconut milk into a bowl and chill in the refrigerator. When quite cold, skim off the thicker 'cream' that rises to the surface, measuring 350 ml (12 fl oz) for the recipe above. The liquid that remains is coconut milk.

23

Steamed Sea Bass

Ca Hap

25 g (1 oz) transparent rice vermicelli
4 dried Chinese mushrooms
4 slices root ginger, cut into small strips
½ teaspoon ground salted black beans
½ white onion, sliced and separated into rings
1 teaspoon sugar
120 ml (4 fl oz) water
1 × 1.5 kg (3 lb) sea bass, gutted and cleaned, or 4 cod cutlets
chopped fresh coriander and basil leaves to serve

Place the vermicelli in a bowl, add warm water to cover and set aside to soak and swell for 15 minutes. Place the dried mushrooms in a second bowl and set aside to soak in warm water for 15 minutes. When both vermicelli and mushrooms are soft, drain both thoroughly. Cut the vermicelli into short lengths and roughly chop the mushrooms.

Combine the vermicelli and mushrooms in a bowl with the ginger, black beans, onion, sugar and water. Mix well.

Place the sea bass or cod cutlets in a shallow ovenproof dish that will fit inside a steamer, then pour the vermicelli mixture over the fish and steam for 10 minutes per 500 g (1 lb), or until the fish flakes easily when tested with a fork.

Transfer the fish and rice vermicelli mixture to a heated platter, sprinkle with fresh coriander and basil leaves and serve immediately.

Fish au Caramel

Ca Bho

500 g (1 lb) firm-fleshed fish, such as salmon, bass or mackerel, cleaned and filleted
5 tablespoons vegetable oil
2 shallots, thinly sliced
2 Chinese white carrots, scraped and thinly sliced
1 piece of root ginger or rhizome, shredded
2 tablespoons nuoc mam (fish gravy)
1 teaspoon black jack (see Note)
½ teaspoon freshly ground black pepper
water (see method)
boiled rice to serve

Cut the cleaned and filleted fish into large pieces at least 5 cm (2 inches) thick.

Heat the oil in a large saucepan, add the shallots and fry until soft but not coloured: this will take about 2 to 3 minutes. Arrange the pieces of fish on top of the softened shallots, tucking the thinly sliced carrots and shredded ginger between them.

Mix the nuoc mam, black jack and pepper in a small bowl. Stir in 4 tablespoons water.

Pour the mixture over the fish, adding extra water to just cover the fish.

Bring the liquid to the boil, lower the heat and simmer very gently, uncovered, for 1 hour, carefully turning the fish over several times. The cooking liquid should gradually reduce to a thick, flavoursome sauce. Serve hot or cold with boiled rice.

Note: Black jack is a strong caramel, sold commercially in jars. If unavailable, heat 1 tablespoon sugar in a heavy bottomed pan until it darkens. Remove the pan from the heat and carefully stir in 2 tablespoons cold water. The mixture may 'spit' at this point so protect hands with oven gloves.

Crabmeat with Asparagus

Thit Cua Xao Mang Tay Hop

12 stalks fresh asparagus
120 ml (4 fl oz) chicken stock
salt
freshly ground black pepper
monosodium glutamate (optional)
1 tablespoon cornflour
2 tablespoons cold water
225 g (8 oz) crabmeat, picked over and flaked
1 egg white, lightly beaten
1¼ teaspoons sesame oil

Peel the thick outer skin from the base of the asparagus stalks and cut the stalks into 2.5 cm (1 inch) lengths. Leave the asparagus tips whole. Bring a saucepan of water to the boil, add the asparagus, lower the heat and simmer gently for 5 to 10 minutes or until the asparagus is tender but still firm.

Meanwhile bring the chicken stock to the boil in a second, smaller saucepan. Season with salt, pepper and monosodium glutamate, if using.

Combine the cornflour and cold water in a cup and mix to a smooth cream. Add to the stock and cook, stirring continuously until it thickens.

Add the crabmeat, lower the heat and simmer for a further 2 minutes.

Stirring gently, add the lightly beaten egg white together with 1 teaspoon of the sesame oil.

Drain the asparagus and divide it between 4 individual bowls or plates. Spoon a portion of crabmeat sauce on to each bowl or plate and finish by adding a few additional drops of sesame oil and sprinkling of pepper. Serve immediately.

Variation: 1 x 340 g (12 oz) can of asparagus spears, drained and cut into 2.5 cm (1 inch) lengths, may be used instead of the stalks of fresh asparagus.

Top left: Steamed Sea Bass; bottom right: Fish au Caramel

Steamed Crabmeat with Water Chestnuts

Thit Cua Hop Voi Ma Thay

225 g (8 oz) cellophane noodles
3 large crabs, cooked
100 g (4 oz) drained canned water chestnuts,
roughly chopped
1 onion, thinly sliced
2 eggs, beaten
salt
freshly ground black pepper
2–3 tablespoons nuoc mam (fish gravy)
1 teaspoon sugar
oil
2 tablespoons chopped fresh coriander leaves to serve

Place the noodles in a large bowl, add warm water to cover and set aside for 15 minutes. Drain and cut into 1 cm (½ inch) lengths. Reserve.

Break the crabs into sections and carefully scrape out all the meat into a large bowl. Add the water chestnuts, noodles, onion and beaten eggs and mix well. Stir in the salt, pepper, nuoc mam and sugar and set aside for 15 minutes.

Generously grease an earthenware pot with oil, add the crabmeat mixture and press it down firmly. Place the pot in the top of a steamer set over boiling water and steam for 15 minutes.

Serve hot, sprinkled with chopped coriander leaves.

Fried Sardines

Ca Sac Din Chien

*4 sardines, cleaned but left whole
5 tablespoons plain flour
1 teaspoon baking powder
1 teaspoon salt
½ teaspoon freshly ground black pepper
1 teaspoon monosodium glutamate (optional)
Oil for deep-frying
2 tablespoons vegetable oil
1 shallot, thinly sliced
1 fresh chilli, seeded and chopped
Nuoc mam giam (see Crispy Spring Rolls, page 14)
to serve*

Pat the sardines dry on paper towels

Combine the flour, baking powder, salt, pepper and monosodium glutamate, if using, in a shallow bowl. Add the fish, turning them in the mixture until coated on all sides. Set aside for 15 minutes.

Heat the oil in a deep-fat fryer. Holding a sardine by the tip of the tail, gently drop into the hot oil, taking care not to allow the hot fat to spatter. If the pan is large enough, add a second sardine in the same way. Deep-fry until all the sardines are golden brown, removing each fish as it cooks and draining on paper towels. Arrange the cooked and drained sardines on a serving platter and keep warm.

Heat the vegetable oil in a small frying pan. Add the shallot and chilli and fry for 3 to 4 minutes until the chopped shallot is golden brown. Pour the mixture over the sardines and serve immediately, with nuoc mam giam as a dipping sauce.

Fried Octopus with Celery and Tomato

Muc Xao Can Tay Voi Ca Chua

*500 g (1 lb) octopus
250 ml (8 fl oz) vegetable oil
5 sticks celery, sliced diagonally into 1 cm
(½ inch) lengths
1–2 cloves garlic, crushed
250 ml (8 fl oz) chicken stock
½ teaspoon salt
½ teaspoon sugar
pinch of monosodium glutamate (optional)
3 tomatoes, skinned and quartered
½ teaspoon cornflour
3 tablespoons water*

*To serve:
fresh coriander leaves
white pepper*

Prepare the octopus. Cut off the tentacles, slice in short lengths and set aside. Clean the octopus by pulling out the intestines and ink sac, then cut out and discard the eyes and beak-like mouth. Score the octopus flesh and cut it neatly into large thin slices. Unless the octopus is very young, it may be necessary to tenderize the slices with a meat mallet.

Heat the oil in a large frying pan, add the octopus and fry gently for 10 minutes. Using a slotted spoon, remove the octopus slices to a plate and reserve.

Add the celery to the oil remaining in the frying pan and cook it briefly (10 seconds will suffice). Remove with a slotted spoon and set aside.

Drain all but 5 tablespoons of oil from the frying pan. To the oil remaining add the crushed garlic with the reserved octopus. Stir-fry for 30 seconds, then stir in the chicken stock, salt, sugar and monosodium glutamate (if using).

Lower the heat and cook for 10 to 15 minutes more or until the octopus is tender. Add the celery and tomatoes, and cook for a further 2 minutes.

Combine the cornflour and water in a cup and mix to a cream. Add to the octopus mixture and cook, stirring constantly, until the sauce thickens.

Transfer the mixture to a serving dish, sprinkle with coriander leaves and white pepper and serve immediately.

Bream with Lemon Grass

Ca Muoi Xa Ot

*1 × 1.75 kg (4 lb) sea bream or haddock, cleaned and
scaled, but with head and tail intact
salt
2 tablespoons finely chopped lemon grass
6 tablespoons vegetable oil
½ teaspoon freshly ground black pepper*

*To serve:
boiled rice
pickled vegetables
nuoc mam giam (see Crispy Spring Rolls, page 14)*

Rub the skin of the bream with salt and rinse thoroughly inside and out with cold running water. Drain and set aside to dry.

Meanwhile, combine the lemon grass, 2 tablespoons oil, ½ teaspoon salt and pepper in a small bowl and mix well.

Score the skin on the back of the fish in several places to allow the sauce to be absorbed while cooking. Rub the lemon grass mixture into the fish, pressing it firmly into the incisions on the back. Place the fish in a shallow dish and set aside for 15 minutes.

Heat the remaining oil in a large frying pan and carefully slide the fish into it. Fry over moderate heat for 10 to 15 minutes, turning carefully once, until the flesh of the fish flakes easily when tested with a fork.

Transfer the fish to a large heated platter and serve immediately with rice, pickled vegetables and nuoc mam giam sauce.

Left: Bream with Lemon Grass; right: Fried Octopus with Celery and Tomato

Grilled Red Mullet

Ca Nuong

50 g (2 oz) transparent rice vermicelli
4 red mullet, gutted and cleaned
salt
1 teaspoon vegetable oil
50 g (2 oz) butter or margarine
2 shallots, finely chopped
2 tablespoons chopped spring onion tops
1 tablespoon ground roasted peanuts

To serve:
1 lettuce, separated into leaves
½ cucumber, thinly sliced
2 tablespoons fresh mint leaves
nuoc mam giam (see Crispy Spring Rolls, page 14)

Bring a large saucepan of water to the boil, add the vermicelli and cook for 3 to 5 minutes until just tender. Drain in a colander, rinse well under cold water and drain again. Arrange the vermicelli on a large platter with the lettuce leaves, cucumber and mint.

Slit each fish down the spine and sprinkle with salt. Arrange on a well-oiled grill rack and cook under a preheated hot grill for 2 minutes on each side. Reduce the temperature to low and cook until the flesh of the fish flakes easily when tested with a fork.

Melt the butter in a small frying pan, add the shallots and spring onion tops and cook, stirring, for 5 seconds.

Transfer the cooked fish to a heated platter, pour the aromatic butter over and sprinkle lightly with ground peanuts. Serve immediately, with the vermicelli and vegetable platter.

Each guest rolls a lettuce leaf around a small portion of fish, vermicelli, cucumber and mint. The filled lettuce rolls are then dipped in nuoc mam giam sauce.

Note: If liked, the nuoc mam giam sauce may be enlivened by the addition of 1 crushed clove garlic and 1 fresh red chilli, seeded and finely chopped.

Variation: For a more formal occasion, dispense with the lettuce, and serve the fish on a bed of rice, with the nuoc mam giam sauce.

Meat & Poultry

Rich, spicy flavourings; texture combinations of crunchiness and tenderness; the aromas of citrus and coriander: these are some of the hallmarks of Vietnamese meat cookery. Chicken responds excellently to this treatment, and a large number of chicken dishes are to be found in this chapter. Beef is used to a greater extent in Vietnam than in its neighbour China, and there are also several game-bird recipes here. The great Asian favourite – pork – features too.

Stewed Chicken with Lemon Grass

Thit Ga Ham Xa

1 × 1.5 kg (3 lb) chicken
5 tablespoons vegetable oil
2 shallots, sliced
6 cloves garlic, crushed
600–750 ml (1–1¼ pints) water
1 teaspoon salt
3 stems lemon grass, finely chopped
3 bay leaves
nuoc mam (fish gravy), salt and freshly ground black pepper to taste
2 tablespoons ground roasted peanuts, to serve

A loaf of French bread makes an excellent accompaniment to this tasty dish.

Bone the chicken and cut into 12 portions.

Heat the oil in a large heavy-bottomed saucepan, add the shallots and garlic and fry over moderate heat for 4 to 5 minutes or until golden brown. Add the chicken and brown on all sides.

Stir in the water, which should just cover the meat, and add the salt, lemon grass and bay leaves. Bring to the boil, lower the heat and simmer for 45 minutes, stirring occasionally.

Season to taste with nuoc mam, salt and freshly ground black pepper and serve immediately, sprinkled with ground roasted peanuts.

Note: If curry leaves are available, use these instead of bay leaves.

Barbecued Chicken in Fermented Bean Curd

Thit Ga Nuong Chao

1 × 1.5 kg (3 lb) tender young chicken
freshly ground black pepper
2 tablespoons vegetable oil
2 tablespoons sesame oil

Marinade:
2 pieces red fermented bean curd
150 g (5 oz) shallots, chopped
8 cloves garlic, crushed
3 tablespoons sugar
1 teaspoon salt
pinch of monosodium glutamate (optional)
2 tablespoons rice alcohol or vodka and 3 cloves, crushed, with 5 cm (2 inches) cinnamon stick

Bone the chicken and cut the flesh into bite-sized pieces.

Combine all the ingredients for the marinade in a shallow dish large enough to hold all the chicken in a single layer. Add the chicken, stir well, sprinkle with pepper and marinate, covered, for 2 hours. Turn the pieces of chicken over from time to time.

Heat the vegetable oil in a large frying pan. Drain the chicken pieces and add them to the pan. Sauté for 2 to 3 minutes until the chicken begins to firm. This is necessary to extract as much liquid as possible from the chicken before grilling.

Arrange the chicken portions on an oiled baking

Left: Stewed Chicken with Lemon Grass; right: Grilled Skewers of Chicken with Five Spices

sheet over medium coals or under a preheated medium grill and cook for 10 minutes, turning frequently.

Brush liberally with sesame oil and cook for 10 to 15 minutes more. Serve immediately.

Grilled Skewers of Chicken with Five Spices

Ga Nuong Ngu Vi Thiong

1 × 1.5 kg (3 lb) tender young chicken

Marinade:
*5 tablespoons vegetable oil
12 shallots, finely chopped
4 cloves garlic, crushed
200 ml (⅓ pint) sake or dry sherry
4 tablespoons soy sauce
1 teaspoon five-spice powder*

To serve:
*boiled rice
green salad*

Bone the chicken and cut the flesh into medium-sized pieces. Place in a shallow dish large enough to hold all the pieces in a single layer.

Make the marinade. Heat the oil in a small saucepan, add the shallots and garlic and cook for 2 to 3 minutes until soft but not coloured. Stir in the remaining ingredients and bring to the boil. Lower the heat and simmer, stirring occasionally, for 4 to 5 minutes. Pour the marinade over the chicken and, using clean hands, gently press the pieces into the liquid to assist absorption. Marinate for at least 30 minutes.

Drain the chicken pieces and spread out on a wire rack to dry, then thread on to 8 metal skewers.

Arrange the chicken kebabs on an oiled grid over medium coals or under a preheated medium grill and brush liberally with the sauce. Cook for 15 to 20 minutes or until golden, turning frequently and brushing several times with the marinade.

Serve with rice and a green salad with French dressing.

Variation: Pork fillet or leg of pork, cut in slices, may be used instead of chicken.

Fried Chicken with Ginger

Thit Ga Chien Gung

1 × 1.5 kg (3 lb) chicken
*1 piece (about 5 cm/2 inches) root ginger, peeled
and shredded*
2 tablespoons white vinegar
5 tablespoons vegetable oil
1 onion, sliced
3 shallots, finely chopped
3 cloves garlic, crushed
2 stems lemon grass, finely chopped
175 ml (6 fl oz) water
1 tablespoon nuoc mam (fish gravy) or to taste
1 teaspoon sugar
freshly ground black pepper to taste
chopped fresh coriander leaves, to serve

Bone the chicken carefully and cut the flesh into small chunks about 1cm – 2cm (½ – ¾ inch) square. Place the peeled and shredded ginger in a small bowl with the vinegar and set aside.

Heat the oil in a large frying pan which has a lid. Add the onion, shallots, garlic and lemon grass and fry, uncovered, over moderate heat for 4 to 5 minutes or until the onion, shallots and garlic are all beginning to turn light brown. Add the chicken chunks to this mixture and stir-fry all together for 3 minutes. Drain off excess oil.

Stir in the reserved ginger and vinegar mixture. Add the water and season to taste with nuoc mam, sugar, and pepper. Add more vinegar to sharpen the flavour, if liked.

Cover the pan and simmer for 10 to 15 minutes, or until the chicken is tender and all the flavours have had a chance to mingle. Serve immediately, sprinkled with coriander leaves and with more pepper, if liked.

Left: Chicken in Spicy Sauce; right: Stir-Fried Chicken with Baby Corn Cobs and Chinese Mushrooms

Chicken in Spicy Sauce

Thit Ga Xao Cay

1 × 1.5 kg (3 lb) tender young chicken
5 tablespoons vegetable oil
6 shallots or 1 large onion, thinly sliced
3 cloves garlic, crushed
6 tomatoes, seeded and chopped
4 teaspoons green peppercorns
2 bay leaves
250 ml (8 fl oz) water
about 1 tablespoon nuoc mam (fish gravy)
salt to taste
about 1 teaspoon sugar
white pepper (optional)

To serve:
boiled rice
1 cucumber, thinly sliced

Bone the chicken and cut the flesh into cubes.

Heat the oil in a large heavy-bottomed saucepan. Add the shallots and garlic and fry over moderate heat for 4 to 5 minutes or until golden brown. Add the chicken and fry, stirring frequently, for 10 minutes.

Stir in the tomatoes, peppercorns, bay leaves and water and bring to the boil. Lower the heat and simmer for 30 minutes or until the sauce is thick.

Stir in the nuoc mam, salt and sugar to taste. Add a little pepper if liked.

Serve immediately, with rice and sliced cucumber.

Stir-fried Chicken with Lemon Grass and Chillies

Ga Xao Xa Ot

4 cloves garlic, chopped
100 g (4 oz) dried shallots
2 teaspoons Malaysian or Thai curry powder
1 teaspoon salt
2 pinches of freshly ground black pepper
1 teaspoon sugar
½ teaspoon monosodium glutamate (optional)
1 kg (2 lb) boneless chicken breast, cut in strips
3 stems lemon grass, finely chopped
2 fresh red chillies, finely chopped
4 tablespoons vegetable oil
120 ml (4 fl oz) water
nuoc mam (fish gravy) to taste
2 tablespoons chopped fresh coriander leaves to serve

The aromatic flavour of lemon grass is a perfect foil for the chillies in this dish.

Using a mortar and pestle, grind 2 of the garlic cloves to a paste with the dried shallots, curry powder, salt, pepper, sugar and monosodium glutamate (if using).

Transfer the mixture to a large bowl, add the chicken strips and stir until well coated. Cover and set aside for 2 hours.

In a second bowl, combine the lemon grass and chillies.

Heat the oil in a large frying pan, add the remaining garlic with the lemon grass and chillies and cook gently for 2 to 3 minutes. Add the chicken strips and stir-fry for 5 minutes.

Stir in the water and bring to the boil. Lower the heat and simmer for 10 to 15 minutes or until the chicken is tender.

Add nuoc mam to taste and sprinkle with additional pepper if liked. Serve immediately, sprinkled with shredded coriander.

Stir-fried Chicken with Baby Corn Cobs and Chinese Mushrooms

Ga Xao Bap Non Va Nam Dong Co

25 g (1 oz) dried Chinese mushrooms
5 tablespoons vegetable oil
2 cloves garlic, crushed
225 g (8 oz) boneless chicken breast, cut in strips
50 g (2 oz) drained canned baby corn cobs
175 ml (6 fl oz) chicken stock
1 tablespoon nuoc mam (fish gravy)
⅓ teaspoon salt
⅓ teaspoon sugar
½ tablespoon cornflour
2 tablespoons water
boiled rice to serve

Place the dried mushrooms in a bowl, add warm water to cover and soak for 15 minutes. Discard the stems and cut each mushroom into quarters.

Heat the oil in a large frying pan, add the garlic and cook over moderate heat until golden. Add the chicken and stir-fry for 10 minutes. With a slotted spoon, transfer the chicken to a plate and set aside.

Add the mushrooms to the oil remaining in the pan, together with the baby corn cobs. Stir-fry for 1 to 2 minutes, then stir in the chicken stock and bring to the boil. Lower the heat, return the chicken to the pan and season with nuoc mam, salt and sugar.

Simmer for 10 minutes or until the chicken is tender and the liquid is reduced by about half.

Combine the cornflour and water in a cup and mix to a cream. Add to the chicken mixture and cook, stirring constantly, until the sauce thickens.

Serve immediately, with rice.

31

Grilled Pigeons

Bo Cau Nuong

2 pigeons, oven-ready
3 tablespoons vegetable oil for grilling

Marinade:
4 cloves garlic, chopped
5 shallots, chopped
1 tablespoon soy sauce
⅓ teaspoon five-spice powder
⅓ teaspoon salt
1 teaspoon sugar
1 tablespoon nuoc mam (fish gravy)
2 tablespoons sake or dry sherry

To serve:
French bread
pickled vegetables

To prepare the pigeons, place them on a wooden board and, using a sharp knife, split each of them down the back. Splay the halves and flatten them with a cleaver.

Make the marinade. Using a mortar and pestle, grind the garlic to a paste with the shallots, soy sauce, five-spice powder, salt and sugar. Stir in the nuoc mam and sake.

Place the pigeons in a large shallow dish and spread the marinade evenly over them. Marinate, covered, for 2 to 4 hours, turning the pigeons several times.

Arrange the pigeons on a well-oiled grid over a pan. Brush with oil and cook under a preheated moderate grill for 20 minutes, turning frequently and brushing with more oil as necessary.

Serve immediately with crusty French bread and pickled vegetables.

Roast Pigeons

Bo Can Ro-ti

4 pigeons, oven-ready
175 ml (6 fl oz) rice alcohol or vodka

Marinade:
5 tablespoons vegetable oil
3 cloves garlic, crushed
½ onion, finely chopped
2 tablespoons soy sauce
2 teaspoons honey or golden syrup
⅓ teaspoon five-spice powder
pinch of freshly ground black pepper
pinch of monosodium glutamate (optional)
6 tablespoons water

Lemon dip:
2 lemons, cut in quarters
2 teaspoons salt
freshly ground black pepper

Prepare the pigeons by rubbing them inside and out

with rice alcohol or vodka. Place on a wire rack and set aside to dry.

Combine all the marinade ingredients and mix thoroughly. Paint the pigeons, inside and out, with this mixture, then leave for about 1 hour to dry. Ideally the birds should be hung in a cool place, but they may be placed on a wire rack.

Arrange the pigeons on a rack in a roasting tin. Brush them liberally with the remaining marinade and roast in a preheated hot oven, 230°C (450°F), Gas Mark 8 for 20 minutes.

Shred the cooked pigeons and arrange the meat on a plate. Divide the lemon wedges between 4 dinner plates, and add ½ teaspoon salt and a pinch of pepper to each. Guests make their own dip by mixing the salt and pepper and moistening the mixture with a squeeze of lemon juice.

Hot and Spicy Quail

Chim Cut Ro-ti

4 quail, oven-ready
3 tablespoons sesame oil for grilling

Marinade:
2 tablespoons vegetable oil
3 cloves garlic, crushed
4 spring onions, finely chopped
1 stem lemon grass, finely chopped
½ teaspoon cayenne pepper
5 drops of Maggi seasoning
1 tablespoon nuoc mam (fish gravy)
1 teaspoon sugar
⅓ teaspoon salt

To serve:
lemon dip (see Roast Pigeons, opposite)
pickled vegetables

To prepare the quail, place them on a wooden board and, using a sharp knife, split each of them down the spine. Splay the halves and flatten them with a cleaver.

Make the marinade. Heat the vegetable oil in a small saucepan, add the garlic, spring onions and lemon grass and cook over moderate heat for 2 to 3 minutes. Leave to cool. Stir in the cayenne, Maggi seasoning, nuoc mam, sugar and salt.

Arrange the quail in a shallow dish large enough to hold them all in a single layer. Pour the marinade over, cover the dish and marinate for 2 hours. Turn the quail over from time to time.

Drain the quail and thread them on to skewers. Arrange on an oiled grid over medium coals or under a preheated moderate grill and brush liberally with sesame oil. Grill for 15 to 20 minutes or until cooked, turning frequently and brushing with more oil as necessary.

Serve immediately, with lemon dip and pickled vegetables.

Left: Roast Pigeons; right: Hot and Spicy Quail

33

Braised Duck

Vit Tim

6 dried Chinese mushrooms
1 × 1.75 kg (4 lb) duck, oven-ready
50 g (2 oz) piece bamboo shoot, sliced
1½ tablespoons soy sauce
2 teaspoons sake or dry sherry
3 spring onions, finely chopped
peel of half an orange

Place the dried mushrooms in a bowl, add warm water to cover and soak for 15 minutes. Discard the stems and cut each mushroom in half. Set aside.

Place the duck in a large saucepan, add boiling water to cover and cook over moderate heat for 10 minutes.

Drain the duck and transfer it to a casserole with the reserved mushrooms, bamboo shoot and soy sauce. Add sufficient water to half cover the duck, cover the casserole and bake in a preheated moderately hot oven, 190°C (375°F), Gas Mark 5 for 1 hour.

Skim off any fat on the surface of the cooking liquid, add the sake or sherry and return the casserole, uncovered, to the oven. Lower the temperature to moderate, 160°C (325°F), Gas Mark 3 and cook for 15 minutes more.

Stir in the spring onions and orange peel and cook for a final 15 to 20 minutes or until the duck is tender and the cooking liquid is well reduced. Serve immediately.

Beef Fondue

Thit Bo Nhung Dam

4 green bananas
500 g (1 lb) fillet steak, thinly sliced
2 cloves garlic, crushed
freshly ground black pepper
1–2 tablespoons vegetable oil
4 star fruit (carambolas), sliced widthways
1 iceberg lettuce, separated into leaves
½ cucumber, sliced
2 tablespoons chopped fresh coriander leaves
2 tablespoons chopped fresh mint leaves
24 sheets banh trang (rice paper)
nuoc mam giam (see Crispy Spring Rolls, page 14)
pickled vegetables

Nuoc mam nem sauce:
5 anchovy fillets
4 tablespoons lemon juice
½ teaspoon sugar or to taste

'Bouillon':
150 ml (¼ pint) flat lemonade
350 ml (12 fl oz) water
2 stems lemon grass
1 large tomato, skinned and seeded
3 tablespoons wine vinegar
3 teaspoons sugar or to taste

34

Slice the green bananas into a bowl of warm water to which 1 teaspoon salt has been added. Set aside for 30 minutes. Meanwhile, arrange the slices of steak on a large platter. Sprinkle with garlic and pepper and brush lightly with oil.

Drain the green bananas and arrange them on a platter with the star fruit, lettuce, cucumber, coriander and mint leaves. Put the banh trang on a separate plate with a large deep bowl of water beside them.

Pour the nuoc mam giam into a small bowl and arrange the pickled vegetables on a plate.

Make the nuoc mam nem by grinding the anchovies to a paste in a mortar with a pestle. Transfer the paste to a bowl and stir in the lemon juice and sugar.

Place a meat fondue set with an adjustable burner in the centre of the table, and arrange the platters of meat, fruit and vegetables and banh trang (with the bowl of water) around it. Add the bowls of sauce and the pickled vegetables.

Prepare the dipping 'bouillon' by combining all the ingredients in the fondue pot. Bring to the boil, either over the fondue flame or on the cooker. Lower the heat and simmer for 1 to 2 minutes. Add sugar to taste if required – the flavour should be sweet and sour.

Transfer the pot to the fondue burner if necessary, adjusting the flame so that the 'bouillon' simmers.

Each guest dunks a banh trang in water to soften it, shakes off the excess liquid and places the banh trang on his plate. He dips a slice of beef in the bouillon until cooked to his taste and places this on the banh trang, adding a selection of trimmings. The banh trang is then rolled and dipped in the sauce of his choice.

Grilled Beef in Vine Leaves

Thit Bo Nuong La Nho

300 g (11 oz) minced steak
3 shallots, finely chopped
4 cloves garlic, crushed
½ teaspoon freshly ground black pepper
½ teaspoon monosodium glutamate (optional)
225 g (8 oz) fresh or drained canned vine leaves
oil for grilling
nuoc mam giam (see Crispy Spring Rolls, page 14)

Mix the minced steak with the shallots, garlic, pepper and monosodium glutamate (if using) in a large bowl, using clean hands to press and mould the mixture together. Set aside for 30 minutes.

Meanwhile, place the vine leaves in a large heatproof bowl. Add boiling water to cover. Allow to stand for 1 minute, then drain. Leave the leaves in the bowl but cover tightly with cling film so they do not dry out.

Place a vine leaf, shiny side down, on the work surface. Trim the stalk. Place a little of the filling in the centre, then turn in the sides to enclose it. Roll up sausage-fashion. Repeat with the remaining leaves.

Arrange the vine leaf parcels on an oiled grid over medium coals or under a preheated moderate grill, and

Left: Grilled Beef with Lemon Grass; right: Grilled Beef in Vine Leaves

brush liberally with oil. Cook for 10 minutes, turning occasionally and brushing with oil as necessary. Serve hot with nuoc mam giam sauce.

Grilled Beef with Lemon Grass

Thit Bo Xao Xa Ot

50 g (2 oz) rice vermicelli
3 cloves garlic, crushed
1 stem lemon grass, finely chopped
2 teaspoons salt
1 teaspoon sugar
½ teaspoon monosodium glutamate (optional)
6 tablespoons oil
500 g (1 lb) fillet steak, thinly sliced
12 sheets banh trang (rice paper)
1 iceberg lettuce, shredded
½ cucumber, sliced
2 tablespoons pickled carrot or radish
1 tablespoon chopped fresh mint
1 tablespoon chopped fresh coriander
nuoc mam giam (see Crispy Spring Rolls, page 14)
2 spring onions, finely chopped
2 tablespoons ground roasted peanuts to serve

Bring a large saucepan of water to the boil, add the vermicelli and cook for 2 to 3 minutes or until tender. Drain in a colander, rinse well and drain again.

Combine the garlic, lemon grass, salt, sugar, monosodium glutamate (if using) and half the oil in a shallow dish large enough to hold all the meat in a single layer. Add the beef and mix well. Cover and marinate for 30 minutes.

Meanwhile, prepare the banh trang by dipping in water. Shake off excess water, roll the banh trang loosely and arrange on a large platter, with the lettuce, cucumber, pickled carrot or radish, mint and coriander.

Place the rice vermicelli in a small bowl, and fill another bowl with nuoc mam giam. Set aside.

Drain the beef slices. Arrange them on an oiled baking sheet over medium coals or under a preheated low to medium grill. Cook for 2 to 3 minutes on each side, or to taste.

Heat the remaining oil in a small saucepan. Place the spring onions in a small heatproof bowl, carefully add the hot oil and mix gently.

Arrange the grilled beef slices on a heated platter and brush with the aromatic oil. Sprinkle with ground roasted peanuts.

Guests make their own banh trang rolls, using a slice of beef and selection of vegetables and vermicelli as the filling for each roll, and dipping the filled rolls in the nuoc mam giam sauce.

Stewed Beef

Thit Bo Kho

4 tablespoons vegetable oil
1 tablespoon Malaysian or Thai curry powder
2 large tomatoes, seeded and finely chopped
1 kg (2 lb) beef shin, cut in 4 cm (1½ inch) cubes
4 large carrots, cut in large chunks
1 onion, quartered
3 star anise
3 bay leaves
2 stems lemon grass, each cut into 3 and crushed
1 beef stock cube
3 tablespoons nuoc mam (fish gravy)
1 teaspoon salt
½ teaspoon freshly ground black pepper
2 teaspoons sugar
French bread to serve

Heat the oil in a large heavy-bottomed saucepan, add the curry powder and tomatoes and cook over gentle heat for 2 minutes, taking care not to let the curry powder scorch.

Stir in the beef, carrots, onion, star anise, bay leaves and lemon grass. Crumble the stock cube over the top and add sufficient water to just cover the meat.

Bring to the boil, lower the heat and simmer for 1 hour, stirring occasionally, until the meat is tender and the liquid has reduced by two-thirds.

Season to taste with nuoc mam, salt, pepper and sugar and serve immediately, with French bread.
Note: The easiest way to seed the tomatoes is to cut them in half and squeeze them gently over a bowl.

Stir-fried Beef with Oyster Sauce

Thit Bo Xao Dau Hao

6 tablespoons vegetable oil
300 g (11 oz) rump steak, thinly sliced
225 g (8 oz) mange tout, trimmed
2 cloves garlic, crushed
120 ml (4 fl oz) chicken stock
3 tablespoons oyster sauce
2 teaspoons cornflour
2 tablespoons water

Heat 4 tablespoons oil in a large frying pan. Add the beef and cook for 2 to 3 minutes until sealed on all sides. With a slotted spoon, transfer the beef slices to a large plate and reserve.

Add the mange tout to the oil remaining in the pan and stir-fry for 2 to 3 minutes. Remove with a slotted spoon and add to the meat.

Pour the remaining oil into the pan if necessary and, when hot, add the garlic. Cook over moderate heat until golden, then return the beef and mange tout to the pan with the stock and oyster sauce. Stir-fry for 5 minutes.

Meanwhile, combine the cornflour and water in a cup and mix to a cream. Add to the mixture and cook, stirring constantly, until the mixture thickens. Serve immediately.

Stir-fried Beef with Bamboo Shoot

Thit Bo Xao Mang

6 tablespoons vegetable oil
300 g (11 oz) rump steak, thinly sliced
3 spring onions, cut in 1 cm (½ inch) lengths
2 cloves garlic, crushed
100 g (4 oz) drained canned bamboo shoot, rinsed and sliced
2 tablespoons nuoc mam (fish gravy)
120 ml (4 fl oz) chicken stock
2 teaspoons sugar
2 teaspoons cornflour
2 tablespoons water

Heat the oil in a large frying pan, add the beef and cook for 2 to 3 minutes until sealed on all sides. With a slotted spoon, transfer the beef slices to a large plate.

Add the spring onions and garlic to the oil remaining in the pan and cook over moderate heat for 3 to 5 minutes or until golden. Increase the heat to high, add the bamboo shoot and stir-fry for 1 minute.

Stir in the nuoc mam, stock and sugar. Cover and cook for 3 minutes, then return the beef to the pan and cook, stirring, for 1 to 2 minutes more.

Meanwhile, combine the cornflour and water in a cup and mix to a cream. Add to the beef mixture and cook, stirring constantly, until the mixture thickens. Serve immediately.

Sweet and Sour Pork Spare Ribs

Suon Heo Chua Ngot

500 g (1 lb) prime pork spare ribs, separated and cut into 5 cm (2 inch) lengths
2 shallots, chopped
3 cloves garlic, crushed
3 tablespoons nuoc mam (fish gravy)
pinch of freshly ground black pepper
1 teaspoon monosodium glutamate (optional)
150 g (5 oz) plain flour
oil for deep-frying

Sweet and sour sauce:
2 pickled onions, sliced
1 onion, diced
2 tablespoons tomato ketchup
4 tablespoons lemon juice
3 tablespoons sugar or to taste
200 ml (⅓ pint) water
vinegar to taste (optional)

Left: Stir-Fried Beef with Oyster Sauce; right: Barbecued Pork Spare Ribs with Lemon Grass

First make the sweet and sour sauce by combining all the ingredients for the sauce in a small saucepan and bringing them to the boil. Lower the heat and simmer, uncovered, for 10 to 15 minutes or until the sauce has reduced to a thick consistency. Allow to cool slightly, taste, and add more sugar or vinegar if necessary to give a balanced sweet and sour flavour. Keep the sauce warm over a low heat until required.

Place the spare ribs in a large heavy-bottomed saucepan with the shallots, garlic, nuoc mam, pepper and monosodium glutamate (if using). Add water to cover. Bring the water to the boil, lower the heat and simmer for 1 hour or until the pork is tender.

Drain the ribs and set aside to cool. Discard the cooking liquid. Spread 4 tablespoons of the flour in a shallow bowl. Place the remaining flour in a second shallow bowl and stir in enough water to form a smooth paste.

Heat the oil in a deep-fat fryer. Roll each spare rib in flour and then dip in the flour paste until well coated. Drop the coated ribs carefully into the hot oil, taking care not to allow the oil to spatter. Cook the coated ribs in several small batches until the coating has turned a delicate golden brown.

As each rib browns, remove it with tongs or a slotted spoon and drain on paper towels. Transfer to a serving dish, pour the sweet and sour sauce over and serve immediately.

Barbecued Pork Spare Ribs with Lemon Grass

Suon Heo Nuong Xa Ot

2 cloves garlic, chopped
1 onion, finely chopped
2 stems lemon grass, finely chopped
⅓ teaspoon five-spice powder
1 teaspoon salt
1 teaspoon freshly ground black pepper
4 tablespoons oil
800 g (1½ lb) prime pork spare ribs, separated

Using a mortar and pestle, grind the garlic, onion and lemon grass to a paste. Stir in the five-spice powder, salt and pepper and bind the mixture with the oil.

Arrange the spare ribs in a single layer in a large shallow dish and cover them with the spice mixture, using clean hands to press the spices into the meat. Cover and set aside for 4 to 6 hours or overnight.

Spread the ribs out on an oiled grid over medium coals or under a preheated medium grill and cook for 15 minutes or until crisp on the outside and tender inside. Alternatively, cook in a preheated moderately hot oven, 190°C (375°F), Gas Mark 5 for 30 minutes.

Bottom Left: Pork and Lettuce Parcels; top right: Caramel Pork

Stir-fried Minced Pork with Bean Curd

Dau Hu Xao Thit Heo Bam

5 tablespoons vegetable oil
4 spring onions, finely chopped
3 slices root ginger, peeled and cut into strips
225 g (8 oz) minced pork
2 tablespoons nuoc mam (fish gravy)
1 teaspoon sugar
pinch of chilli powder
120 ml (4 fl oz) chicken stock
4 pieces bean curd, each piece cut into 4 cubes
1 teaspoon cornflour
2 tablespoons water

Heat the oil in a saucepan, add half the spring onions and all the ginger and fry over moderate heat for 4 to 5 minutes or until golden brown. Add the minced pork, nuoc mam, sugar and chilli powder and stir-fry for 4 to 6 minutes.

Stir in the chicken stock and bring to the boil. Lower the heat and simmer for 10 minutes, stirring gently from time to time.

Add the bean curd and cook for 1 minute more, stirring gently.

Combine the cornflour and water in a cup and mix to a cream. Add to the pork mixture and cook, stirring gently until the mixture thickens.

Sprinkle with the remaining spring onions and serve immediately.

Marinated Roast Lean Pork

Xa Xiu

500 g (1 lb) pork fillet, cut lengthways in long 5 cm (2 inch) wide strips
2 tablespoons chopped pickled cucumber to serve

Marinade:
3 shallots, finely chopped
1 teaspoon salt
½ teaspoon freshly ground black pepper
1 teaspoon sugar
1 teaspoon monosodium glutamate (optional)
1–2 drops red food colouring
5 tablespoons sake or dry sherry

Combine all the ingredients for the marinade in a shallow dish large enough to hold all the pork in a single layer. Mix well.

Add the pork strips, turning to coat them in the mixture. Cover and marinate for 3 hours in the refrigerator, turning the pork strips occasionally.

Arrange the pork strips on a wire rack set over a roasting tin half filled with cold water. Place the tin in a preheated moderate oven, 160°C (325°F), Gas Mark 3 and bake for 30 minutes or until the pork strips are tender.

Cut the pork strips into shorter lengths and arrange on a heated platter. Sprinkle with chopped pickled cucumber and serve immediately.

Pork and Lettuce Parcels

Thit Heo Cuon Hanh Huong

1 bunch spring onions, green tops only
500 g (1 lb) lean belly of pork
3 slices root ginger, peeled
1 lettuce, separated into leaves
½ cucumber, sliced
2 tablespoons chopped fresh mint
2 tablespoons chopped fresh coriander
nuoc mam giam (see Crispy Spring Rolls, page 14) to serve

These pretty parcels, tied with spring onion green, are a popular summer speciality in Vietnam.

Place the spring onion tops in a heatproof bowl, pour boiling water over and allow to stand for 1 minute. Drain and reserve.

Combine the pork and ginger in a large saucepan. Add water to cover. Bring to the boil, lower the heat and simmer for 45 minutes to 1 hour or until the pork is tender. Drain the pork. When cool enough to handle, cut in thin 3 mm (⅛ inch) strips. Allow to cool completely.

Blanch the lettuce leaves to make them pliable. Spread out a lettuce leaf on a wooden board or clean work surface. Top with a couple of pork shreds, 1 or 2 cucumber slices and a little mint and coriander. Fold to a neat parcel and secure with a length of spring onion green, tying it in a neat bow.

Arrange the parcels on a serving platter with a bowl of nuoc mam giam in the centre as a dip. Serve cold.

Caramel Pork

Thit Heo Kho

50 g (2 oz) sugar
water (see method)
500 g (1 lb) leg of pork, cut into large cubes
3 white radishes (daikon), peeled and thinly sliced
½ onion, chopped
5 tablespoons nuoc mam (fish gravy)
½ teaspoon freshly ground black pepper
boiled rice to serve

Place the sugar in a large heavy-bottomed saucepan and heat gently until it begins to smell burnt. Stir in 2 tablespoons water (take care as the mixture may 'spit').

Add the pork and the radishes and top up with sufficient water to cover the meat. Add the remaining ingredients, bring to the boil, then reduce the heat and simmer for 45 minutes to 1 hour, or until the pork is cooked and the liquid is reduced to one third of its original quantity.

Serve hot with rice.

Eggs Rice & Noodles

Rice and noodles are of almost equal importance in Vietnamese cookery, though each plays a different role within Vietnam's eating day. Noodles are primarily snack or light meal food – they're a lunchtime favourite, for example – while rice, particularly the plain boiled variety, is more important as an accompaniment to fish, meat or vegetable dishes. This chapter also contains a number of egg recipes which make excellent lunchtime fare.

40

Plain Boiled Rice

Com Trang

225 g (8 oz) long-grain rice
300 ml (½ pint) water
1 teaspoon salt

In Vietnam, rice is cooked in a small amount of water, which is absorbed during cooking leaving the grains dry and separate. The Vietnamese method of measuring the amount of water required is to dip the index finger into the saucepan of rice. When the tip of the finger touches the surface of the rice, the water level should reach halfway up to the first joint (about 1cm/½ inch). The quantities listed above will give the same results.

Wash the rice several times in cold water and drain thoroughly before cooking. Place the rice in a heavy-bottomed saucepan with the salt and the water and bring to the boil. Stir with a fork and cook over medium to high heat until most of the water has been absorbed (about 3 minutes).

Lower the heat, cover the pan and simmer very gently without stirring for 12 to 15 minutes or until the rice is tender but still firm to the bite.

The rice may be served immediately, or placed in a covered bowl in the refrigerator for up to 3 days for use in fried rice dishes.

Fried Rice with Egg

Com Chien Trung

2 eggs
2 tablespoons water
6 tablespoons vegetable oil
2 spring onions, finely chopped
plain boiled rice (see previous recipe)
2 tablespoons soy sauce
½ teaspoon salt
½ teaspoon sugar
pinch of monosodium glutamate (optional)

Beat the eggs with the water in a small bowl. Heat 1 tablespoon of the oil in a small frying pan, add the egg mixture and swirl to make an omelette. Lower heat.

Using a spatula or round-bladed knife, lift the sides of the omelette to allow any uncooked egg to flow underneath. As soon as the omelette is cooked, slip it on to a plate. When cool, cut into strips.

Heat the remaining oil in a large frying pan (preferably non-stick). Add the spring onions and fry for 2 minutes, stirring, then add the rice and omelette strips. Stir in the soy sauce, salt, sugar and monosodium glutamate (if using).

Cook, stirring, for 2 to 3 minutes until the mixture is dry. Serve immediately.

Left: Fried Rice with Eggs; right: Special Fried Rice

Special Fried Rice

Com Chien Thap Cam

2 Chinese sausages
2 eggs
2 tablespoons water
6 tablespoons vegetable oil
1 shallot, finely chopped
50 g (2 oz) ham, diced
25 g (1 oz) shrimps
plain boiled rice (see recipe opposite)
2 tablespoons soy sauce
½ teaspoon sugar
½ teaspoon salt
pinch of monosodium glutamate (optional)

Place the Chinese sausages in the top of a steamer over boiling water. Steam for 15 minutes, then allow to cool slightly. Slice thinly and set aside.

Beat the eggs with the water in a small bowl.

Heat 1 tablespoon of the oil in a small frying pan, add the egg mixture and swirl the pan to make an omelette. Lower the heat.

Using a spatula or round-bladed knife, lift the sides of the omelette to allow any uncooked egg to flow underneath. As soon as the omelette is cooked, flip it on to a plate. When cool, cut into strips.

Heat the remaining oil in a large frying pan (preferably non-stick). Add the shallot and fry for 2 minutes, stirring, then add all the other remaining ingredients. Cook, stirring, for 2 to 3 minutes. Serve immediately.

Left: Fried Rice Noodles with Beef and Green Pepper; right: Fried Crispy Noodles with Chicken, Ham and Prawns

42

Fresh Egg Noodles

Mi Vat Tuoi

**500 g (1 lb) fresh egg noodles
pinch of salt
water**

Fresh egg noodles are available from Oriental grocery stores and are usually sold by weight. They are used as an accompaniment or in soups.

Bring a large saucepan of salted water to the boil. Add the noodles and boil, stirring constantly, for 8 to 10 minutes or until tender but still firm to the bite.

Drain in a colander, rinse with boiling water and drain again. Serve as an accompaniment, or with bouillon as a tasty soup.

Dried Egg Noodles

Mi Vat Kho

**4 bundles dried egg noodles
pinch of salt
boiling water**

Dried egg noodles are sold prepackaged in bundles, and 1 bundle should be allowed per person. They are mainly used for frying, but have to be boiled first and require a slightly different cooking method from fresh noodles.

Place the bundles of noodles in a large saucepan with a pinch of salt, and pour over boiling water to cover. Allow to stand for 5 minutes.

Bring the liquid back to the boil and cook the noodles, stirring constantly, for 4 to 5 minutes or until tender but still firm to the bite. Drain in a colander, rinse with cold water and drain again.

Allow to dry slightly before frying.

Fried Rice Noodles with Beef and Green Pepper

Pho Xao Thit Bo Va Ot Xanh

6 tablespoons vegetable oil
225 g (8 oz) rice noodles
½ onion, sliced
3 cloves garlic, crushed
2 green peppers, cored, seeded and cut into chunks
500 g (1 lb) fillet steak, thinly sliced
300 ml (½ pint) chicken stock
1 tablespoon nuoc mam (fish gravy)
1 teaspoon dark soy sauce
3 teaspoons salt
⅓ teaspoon sugar
1 tablespoon cornflour
2 tablespoons water
freshly ground black pepper

To serve:
spring onion tops, cut into fine strips

Fresh rice noodles are best for this dish, but dried ones will do. Look for the product with the Vietnamese words 'banh pho' or 'hu tieu' on the wrapper. Cook them as you would dried egg noodles (see page 42), then rinse under cold water and allow to drain for 8 to 10 minutes until dry.

Heat the oil in a large frying pan (preferably non-stick). When it starts to smoke, add the cooked noodles carefully, spreading them out in the pan. Treat them very gently – they are much more fragile than the egg noodle.

Cook for 3 minutes, stirring, then pat the noodles firmly into a pancake shape and allow this to brown lightly. When the first side is browned, carefully turn the noodle pancake over and cook the other side in the same way. Remove from the pan and drain on paper towels.

Add the onion and garlic to the oil remaining in the pan and stir-fry for 3 to 5 minutes or until light golden in colour. Add the green peppers and beef and stir-fry quickly for 1 minute, then stir in the stock.

Add nuoc mam, dark soy sauce, salt and sugar to taste and mix well so that all the ingredients are thoroughly combined.

Combine the cornflour and cold water in a cup and mix carefully to a smooth cream. Add this mixture to the sauce and continue to cook, stirring constantly until it thickens.

Place the noodles on a large serving platter. Top with the sauce and sprinkle with freshly ground black pepper. Decorate with fine strips of spring onion and serve immediately.

Fried Crispy Noodles with Chicken, Ham and Prawns

Mi Xao Gion

6 dried Chinese mushrooms
6 tablespoons vegetable oil
cooked dried noodles (see recipe opposite)
½ onion, sliced
1 boneless chicken breast, cut into strips
12 raw shelled prawns, deveined (see Transparent Spring Rolls, page 13)
2 slices cooked ham, cut into strips
25 g (1 oz) piece bamboo shoot, cut into strips
300 ml (½ pint) chicken stock
1 tablespoon nuoc mam (fish gravy)
⅓ teaspoon salt
⅓ teaspoon sugar
1 tablespoon cornflour
2 tablespoons water
2 tablespoons chopped fresh coriander to serve

Place the dried Chinese mushrooms in a small bowl, add warm water to cover and set aside to soak and swell for 15 to 20 minutes. Drain the mushrooms thoroughly, cut off and discard their stems and cut each mushroom cap into quarters.

Heat the oil in a large frying pan (preferably non-stick). When it starts to smoke, add the noodles carefully, spreading them out in the pan.

Cook for 3 minutes, stirring gently, then pat the noodles firmly into a pancake shape and allow to brown slightly. Turn the pancake of noodles over and brown the other side. Remove and drain on paper towels.

Add the sliced onion, strips of chicken breast and prepared prawns to the oil remaining in the pan and stir-fry quickly for 2 to 3 minutes.

Stir in the strips of ham and bamboo shoot, mix well and stir-fry for 1 minute more. Add the chicken stock, nuoc mam, salt and sugar and cook for a further 2 minutes, stirring as you do so.

Combine the cornflour and cold water in a cup and mix carefully to a smooth cream. Add this mixture to the sauce and continue to cook, stirring constantly, until it thickens.

Place the noodles on a large serving platter, top with the chicken, ham and prawn sauce and sprinkle with coriander. Serve immediately.

43

Fried Noodles with Bean Sprouts

Mi Xao Gia

4 tablespoons oil
200 g (7 oz) fresh bean sprouts
2 tablespoons chopped spring onions
cooked dried noodles (see Dried Egg Noodles, page 42)
sugar, soy sauce and salt to taste
2–3 drops sesame oil

Heat the oil in a large frying pan (preferably non-stick) and add the bean sprouts. Stir-fry for 2 to 3 minutes.

Add the spring onions and noodles, raise the heat to high and stir-fry until all the liquid has evaporated.

Remove from the heat and season to taste with sugar, soy sauce and salt. Sprinkle with a few drops of sesame oil and serve immediately.

Variation: 1 tablespoon oyster sauce may be used instead of sesame oil if preferred.

Noodles with Pacific Prawns

Mi Xao Tom

25 g (1 oz) dried Chinese mushrooms
500 g (1 lb) raw Pacific prawns, shelled and deveined (8 oz Transparent Spring Rolls, page 13) and cut in half lengthways
salt
100 g (4 oz) fresh noodles
6 tablespoons vegetable oil
1 onion, finely chopped
1 green pepper, cored, seeded and cut in diamonds
1 carrot, diced
1 stick celery, diced
120 ml (4 fl oz) chicken stock
1 tablespoon nuoc mam (fish gravy)
1 teaspoon sugar
1 teaspoon dark soy sauce
1 tablespoon cornflour
2 tablespoons water
freshly ground black pepper

Place the mushrooms in a small bowl with warm water to cover. Soak for 15 minutes, then drain thoroughly and slice thinly.

Wash the prawns and dry on paper towels.

Bring a large saucepan of salted water to the boil. Add the noodles and cook, stirring constantly, for 8 to 10 minutes or until tender but still firm to the bite. Drain in a colander, rinse with boiling water and drain again. Spread out on a large clean tea towel to dry.

Heat the oil in a large frying pan, add the prawns and fry for 30 seconds. Stir in the noodles and cook for 2 to 3 minutes more until the prawns are pink and the noodles crisp and separate. With a slotted spoon remove the prawns and noodles from the pan and arrange on a platter. Keep warm.

Add the onion to the oil remaining in the pan and cook for 3 to 4 minutes or until golden brown. Stir in the mushrooms, green pepper, carrot and celery and stir-fry for 30 to 45 seconds. Moisten the mixture with the chicken stock and season with nuoc mam, sugar and dark soy sauce.

Combine the cornflour and water in a cup and mix to a cream. Stir into the vegetable mixture. Simmer, stirring constantly until the sauce thickens. Simmer for 2 minutes more.

Pour the sauce over the noodles and prawns, sprinkle with pepper and serve immediately.

Rice Vermicelli

Bun

500 g (1 lb) rice vermicelli
salt
water

Vietnamese cooks make great use of vermicelli, both as an accompaniment to main course dishes in its own right, and as the basis of a wide range of soups, salads and savoury dishes. Rice vermicelli, in particular, is a hallmark of authentic Vietnamese cookery, and anyone who wishes to cook true Vietnamese food should make every effort to obtain a supply of this ingredient.

Great care should be taken in cooking rice vermicelli. It is a delicate item, and careless cooking will impair its eating qualities. If the instructions below are followed carefully, however, excellent results will be obtained.

Bring a large saucepan of salted water to the boil. Add the rice vermicelli and boil, stirring constantly, for 3 to 5 minutes or until the vermicelli is tender but still firm to the bite.

Drain the vermicelli in a colander and rinse under cold running water to remove excess starch. Drain once again thoroughly.

If serving as part of a composite dish, halve the quantity of vermicelli given above.

If the vermicelli is to be served as an accompaniment, rinse with boiling water to reheat it just before it is required for serving.

If the vermicelli is to be part of a composite dish, spread it out and allow to dry for 30 or so minutes before combining it with the other ingredients.

For dishes requiring fried rice vermicelli, prepare the vermicelli by soaking it in warm water for 15 minutes, then drain thoroughly in a colander and allow to dry for 15 minutes.

Transparent rice vermicelli should be prepared for frying in the same way.

Left: Fried Noodles with Bean Sprouts; right: Rice Vermicelli with Barbecued Pork

45

Rice Vermicelli with Barbecued Pork

Bun Thit Heo Nuong

2 cloves garlic, crushed
2 spring onions, roughly chopped
1 teaspoon black jack (see Fish au Caramel, page 24)
½ teaspoon salt
½ teaspoon freshly ground black pepper
300 g (11 oz) pork belly, sliced and cut into squares
1 iceberg lettuce, shredded
½ cucumber, sliced
2 tablespoons pickled carrots or gherkins
1 tablespoon fresh mint leaves
1 tablespoon chopped fresh coriander leaves
50 g (2 oz) rice vermicelli, cooked (see opposite)
8 tablespoons nuoc mam giam or to taste (see Crispy Spring Rolls, page 14)

Combine the garlic, spring onions and black jack in a shallow dish large enough to hold all the thin squares of pork in a single layer. Add salt and pepper and the pork. Mix well, cover and set aside to marinate for at least 30 minutes.

Meanwhile, prepare the lettuce, cucumber, pickled vegetables, mint and coriander leaves and divide between 4 individual bowls. Top each portion of vegetables with cooked vermicelli. Set aside.

Place the marinated pork squares on a baking sheet and cook over medium coals or under a preheated moderate grill for 15 to 20 minutes, turning once during the cooking period.

Divide the barbecued pork slices between the bowls and top each with 2 tablespoons nuoc mam giam, or to taste.

Each guest mixes the contents of his or her bowl thoroughly before eating.

Chicken and Rice Hotpot

Com Ga

500 g (1 lb) long-grain rice (see method)
25 g (1 oz) dried Chinese mushrooms
1 × 2 kg (4 lb) roasting chicken
900 ml (1½ pints) water

Marinade:
3 tablespoons sake or dry sherry
1 teaspoon sugar
2 teaspoons cornflour
1 teaspoon salt
1 teaspoon sesame oil
1 tablespoon soy sauce
1 teaspoon monosodium glutamate (optional)

Sauce:
2 tablespoons vegetable oil
50 g (2 oz) dried shallots
2 tablespoons Maggi seasoning
1 teaspoon sugar
120 ml (4 fl oz) chicken stock
½ teaspoon monosodium glutamate (optional)

Aromatic rice would be used for this dish in Vietnam, although ordinary long-grain rice is perfectly acceptable.

Wash the rice thoroughly several times in cold water and drain thoroughly. Place the mushrooms in a small bowl with warm water to cover. Soak for 15 minutes, then drain thoroughly and cut each piece into quarters.

Remove the chicken flesh from the carcass and cut into small cubes. Place in a shallow bowl large enough to hold all the cubes in a single layer.

Place the carcass in a large saucepan with the measured water and bring to the boil. Cook for 30 minutes.

Add the mushrooms to the chicken cubes. Mix all the ingredients for the marinade and add to the bowl. Stir to coat the chicken and mushrooms thoroughly. Set aside for 30 minutes.

Place the rice in a hotpot or heavy-bottomed saucepan with a lid. Measure 750 ml (1¼ pints) of the chicken stock and add. Bring the liquid to the boil. Lower the heat, cover the hotpot or pan and simmer for 10 minutes.

Stir in the chicken and mushrooms, with the marinade. Mix well. Replace the lid and simmer for 15 minutes more, or until both the rice and the chicken are cooked.

Just before serving, prepare the sauce. Heat the oil

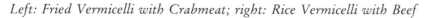

Left: Fried Vermicelli with Crabmeat; right: Rice Vermicelli with Beef

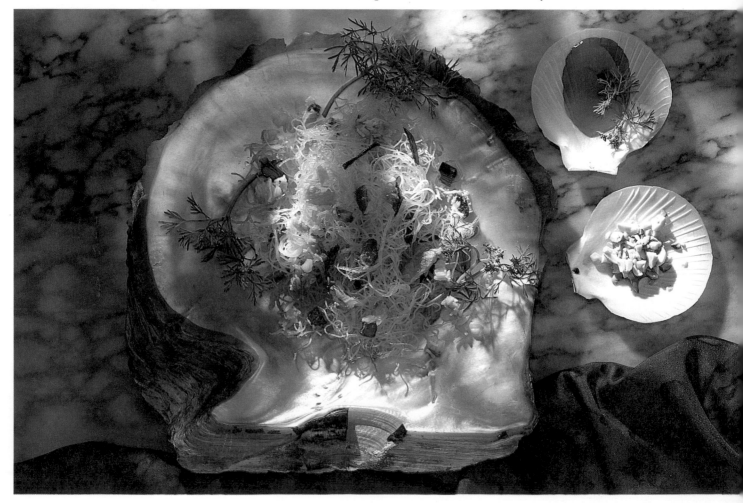

in a small saucepan, add the shallots and fry for 1 minute. Stir in the Maggi seasoning, sugar, salt, stock and monosodium glutamate, if using. Bring to the boil and cook, stirring occasionally, for 1 minute.

Pour the sauce over the chicken and rice mixture and serve at once.

Rice Vermicelli with Beef

Bun Bo

2 cloves garlic, crushed
1 onion, sliced
1 stem lemon grass, finely chopped
½ teaspoon salt
⅓ teaspoon freshly ground black pepper
6 tablespoons nuoc mam (fish gravy)
½ teaspoon sugar
500 g (1 lb) fillet steak, finely sliced
100 g (4 oz) bean sprouts
1 iceberg lettuce, shredded
2 tablespoons sliced pickled carrots or gherkins
1 tablespoon fresh mint leaves
100 g (4 oz) rice vermicelli, cooked (see page 45)
4 tablespoons vegetable oil
1 tablespoon crushed roasted peanuts to serve

This dish, a sort of hot and cold salad, has a refreshing combination of textures and flavours. It is made in three distinct layers and topped with sauce. Each guest mixes all the components in his or her bowl together just before eating.

Combine the garlic, onion, lemon grass, salt, pepper, 2 tablespoons nuoc mam and sugar in a shallow dish large enough to hold all the beef in a single layer. Add the beef, mix well, cover and marinate for 30 minutes.

Meanwhile, prepare the bean sprouts, lettuce, pickled vegetables and mint leaves and divide between 4 individual bowls. Top each portion of vegetables with cooked vermicelli. Set aside.

Heat the oil in a large frying pan, add the beef and stir-fry for 2 to 4 minutes on each side or until done to your taste.

Add a portion of steak to each bowl, top each with 1 tablespoon of the remaining nuoc mam and sprinkle with roasted peanuts. Serve immediately.

Fried Vermicelli with Crabmeat

Mien Xao Cua

100 g (4 oz) transparent rice vermicelli, prepared for frying (see page 45)
5–7 tablespoons oil
3 spring onions, roughly chopped
100 g (4 oz) fresh or canned crabmeat, picked over and flaked
3–4 tablespoons chicken stock
1 teaspoon salt
2 tablespoons nuoc mam (fish gravy)
¼ teaspoon monosodium glutamate (optional)

To serve:
freshly ground black pepper
2 tablespoons chopped fresh coriander

Prepare the transparent rice vermicelli as described on page 45. Spread out and leave to dry.

Heat 5 tablespoons oil in a large frying pan (preferably non-stick), add the spring onions and fry over low to medium heat for 3 to 5 minutes until the white portions are lightly coloured.

Stir in the crabmeat and vermicelli, with more oil if necessary, and stir-fry for 2 minutes more. If the mixture is very dry, moisten it with the chicken stock and cook for about 5 minutes or until the vermicelli is soft and all the strands are separate.

Season with salt and nuoc mam, adding the monosodium glutamate, if using.

Sprinkle with pepper and coriander tops and serve immediately.

Chicken and Mushroom Omelette

Omelette Ga Voi Nam

15 g (½ oz) dried Chinese mushrooms
4 eggs
2 tablespoons chicken stock or water
100 g (4 oz) smoked or roast chicken, shredded
50 g (2 oz) baked ham, cut into thin matchsticks
1 spring onion bulb, thinly sliced
salt
freshly ground black pepper
½ teaspoon sake or dry sherry (optional)
5 tablespoons vegetable oil
1 tomato, thinly sliced, to serve

Place the mushrooms in a small bowl with warm water to cover. Soak for 15 minutes, then drain and slice thinly. Reserve.

Beat the eggs with the chicken stock in a medium bowl. Stir in the chicken, ham, mushrooms and spring onion. Season to taste with salt and pepper and add the rice wine, if using.

Heat the oil in a large frying pan (preferably non-stick). When it is very hot, add the egg mixture and swirl the pan to make an omelette. Lower the heat.

Using a spatula or round-bladed knife, lift the sides of the omelette to allow any uncooked egg to flow underneath. When the omelette is almost cooked, roll it up and slice it on to a serving plate. Decorate with the sliced tomato and serve immediately.

48

Quail Eggs with Straw Mushrooms and Bamboo Shoots

Trung Cut Xao Nam Va Mang

20 quail eggs
dark soy sauce (see method)
100 g (4 oz) watercress, washed
5 tablespoons vegetable oil
1 small onion, roughly chopped
3 cloves garlic, finely chopped
1 carrot, diced
1 large piece (about 100 g/4 oz) bamboo shoot, diced
100 g (4 oz) drained canned straw mushrooms
120 ml (4 fl oz) chicken stock
1 tablespoon cornflour
3 tablespoons water
salt
freshly ground black pepper
1 teaspoon light soy sauce
1 teaspoon sesame oil

Place the quail eggs in a saucepan with cold water to cover. Bring the water to the boil, cook for 1 minute, then drain the eggs. Crack the shells all over with a spoon and remove very carefully so as not to damage the eggs.

Return the eggs to the clean saucepan and cover with equal quantities of water and dark soy sauce. Bring to the boil, lower the heat and simmer for 20 minutes.

Bring a large saucepan of water to the boil, add the watercress and blanch for 1 minute. Drain, refresh under cold water and drain again, blotting excess moisture with paper towels. Arrange the watercress on a large platter.

Heat the oil in a large frying pan and add the onion and garlic. Fry for 3 to 4 minutes until golden brown. Stir in the carrot, bamboo shoot, straw mushrooms and chicken stock and simmer for 1 minute.

Meanwhile combine the cornflour and water in a cup and mix to a cream. season the vegetable mixture with salt, pepper and light soy sauce. Add the cornflour mixture and cook, stirring, until the sauce thickens.

Return the quail eggs to the frying pan with the sesame oil and heat through gently for 1 minute.

Spoon the mixture on to the bed of watercress. Serve immediately.

Steamed Eggs with Minced Pork

Trung Hap Thit Heo

25 g (1 oz) cellophane noodles
15 g (½ oz) wood ear
5 eggs
3 tablespoons water
75 g (3 oz) minced pork
1 small shallot, finely chopped
¼ teaspoon freshly ground black pepper
½ teaspoon sugar
1 tablespoon nuoc mam (fish gravy)
nuoc mam giam (see Crispy Spring Rolls, page 14)
to serve

Place the noodles and wood ear in a bowl, add warm water to cover and set aside for 15 minutes. Drain and chop both the noodles and the wood ear roughly.

Beat the eggs with the water in a large bowl. Add the pork, noodles, wood ear and shallot. Season to taste with pepper, sugar and nuoc mam.

Pour the egg mixture into a heatproof bowl that will fit inside a steamer. Steam over boiling water for 15 minutes or until the mixture is set. Test by inserting a chopstick into the mixture. If no liquid runs out, the egg mixture is cooked.

Serve immediately, with nuoc mam giam. Fresh chopped chilli and pepper may also be offered.

Left: Chicken and Mushroom Omelette; right: Quail Eggs with Straw Mushrooms and Bamboo Shoots

Crabmeat Omelettes

Trang Trung Voi Cua

25 g (1 oz) cellophane noodles
15 g (½ oz) wood ear
4 eggs
300 g (11 oz) crabmeat, picked over and flaked
50 g (2 oz) dried shallots
salt
freshly ground black pepper
pinch of monosodium glutamate (optional)
6 tablespoons vegetable oil

Place the noodles and wood ear in a bowl, add warm water to cover and set aside for 15 minutes. Drain and chop both the noodles and the wood ear finely.

Beat the eggs in a large bowl, add the crabmeat, noodles, wood ear and shallots and mix well. Season with salt, pepper and monosodium glutamate (if using). The mixture should be fairly stiff.

Heat the oil in a large frying pan (preferably non-stick). Divide the crabmeat mixture into 4 equal portions. Form each into a shallow cake. Slide the cakes into the frying pan. As each underside turns brown, flip the omelette cakes over and cook the other side. Serve immediately.

Salads & Vegetables

The recipes in this chapter, in addition to being excellent accompaniments to many fish and meat recipes, would also compose a number of memorable vegetarian meals. Vietnamese vegetable cooking is full of contrasts: there are both light dishes and rich dishes, and colours and textures are pleasantly varied, so the potential for experiment is good.

Stir-fried Mixed Vegetables

Rau Xao

25 g (1 oz) wood ears (dry weight)
2 carrots, finely sliced
100 g (4 oz) piece bamboo shoot, thinly sliced
1 Chinese cabbage (Bok choy), stems only, diced
100 g (4 oz) green beans, halved
4 tablespoons vegetable oil
2 cloves garlic, crushed
2–3 slices root ginger, peeled and cut in slivers
100 g (4 oz) bean sprouts
½ teaspoon salt
½ teaspoon freshly ground black pepper
pinch of monosodium glutamate (optional)
1 teaspoon cornflour
1 tablespoon water

Place the wood ears in a small bowl. Add warm water to cover and set aside for 15 minutes. Drain thoroughly and chop roughly. Set aside.

Bring a large saucepan of water to the boil. Add the carrots and cook for 10 minutes. Add the bamboo shoot, Chinese cabbage and green beans and cook for 5 minutes more. Drain thoroughly and reserve.

Heat the oil in a wok or large frying pan, add the garlic and ginger and stir-fry for 2 minutes. Add the bean sprouts and stir-fry for 30 seconds.

Stir in all the reserved vegetables, including the wood ears, and season with salt, pepper and monosodium glutamate (if using). Stir-fry for 1 to 2 minutes more. The vegetables should remain crisp.

Combine the cornflour and water in a cup and mix to a cream. Add to the wok and stir constantly to bind the vegetables together. Serve immediately.

Crispy Bean Curd with Tomato Sauce

Dau Hu Rau Voi Sot Ca Chua

oil for deep-frying
6 pieces bean curd, halved then cut into small triangles
3 large tomatoes, skinned, seeded and finely chopped
150 ml (¼ pint) chicken stock
1 tablespoon nuoc mam (fish gravy)
pinch of salt
⅓ teaspoon sugar
2 spring onion tops, cut into fine strips, to serve

Heat the oil in a deep-fat fryer or wok, add the bean curd and fry until golden brown. Remove with a slotted spoon and set aside.

Place the tomatoes in a medium saucepan with the chicken stock, nuoc mam, salt and sugar. Bring to the boil, lower the heat and simmer for 15 to 20 minutes.

Add the bean curd and simmer for 10 to 15 minutes more. The sauce should be quite thick and flavoursome. Sprinkle with the fine strips of spring onion and serve immediately.

Left: Crispy Bean Curd with Tomato Sauce; right: Stir-fried Mixed Vegetables

51

Vegetarian Spring Roll

Cha Gio Chay

100 g (4 oz) yellow mung beans, washed
oil for deep frying
2 large pieces of bean curd
50 g (2 oz) canned water chestnut, chopped
50 g (2 oz) cellophane noodles, soaked in
water then chopped coarsely
20 g (¾ oz) wood ears (dry weight),
soaked in water then chopped coarsely
3 cloves garlic, chopped
2 carrots, grated finely
½ teaspoon ground pepper
2 teaspoons salt
20 sheets banh trang (rice paper)
water or beaten egg to seal
light soy sauce, to serve

Soak the mung beans in a large bowl of water for several hours. Drain, then steam them for 30 minutes or until soft. Place the mung beans in a food processor and work until they form a smooth paste.

Heat the oil in a deep-fat fryer or wok, add the bean curd and fry until golden brown. Remove with a slotted spoon and set aside. When cool, cut into fine strips.

Put the remainder of the ingredients (excluding the banh trang) in a large mixing bowl and add the mung bean paste. Mix well.

Dip the sheets of banh trang in cold water, carefully shake off excess water, and lay the sheets on a clean work surface. Divide the mung bean mixture between them, piling it along one end of each sheet, about 2.5 cm (1 inch) from the end and a similar distance from the sides. Scatter the strips of bean curd over the filling. Turn the sides of the banh trang over the filling, then roll up, sausage-fashion. Seal the ends with a little water or beaten egg.

Reheat the oil in the deep-fat fryer or wok. Add the rolls, a few at a time, and deep-fry until golden brown. Drain on paper towels and serve immediately, with light soy sauce as a dip.

Sweet-and-Sour Chinese Mushrooms

Nam Dong Co Chua Ngot

50 g (2 oz) dried Chinese mushrooms
plain flour
oil for frying
1 carrot, cut into fine strips
50 g (2 oz) white of spring onions, cut into fine strips
2 sticks of celery, sliced diagonally into 1 cm (½ inch) lengths
3 cloves garlic, chopped
salt
freshly ground black pepper
monosodium glutamate (optional)
fresh coriander, to serve

Sweet-and-sour sauce:
2 pickled onions, sliced
1 onion, diced
2 tablespoons tomato ketchup
4 tablespoons lemon juice
3 tablespoons sugar or to taste
200 ml (7 fl oz) water
vinegar to taste (optional)

Soak the Chinese mushrooms in water for 30 minutes, while you make the sauce.

To make the sweet and sour sauce, combine all the ingredients in a small saucepan and bring them to the boil. Lower the heat and simmer, uncovered, for 10 to 15 minutes until the sauce has reduced to a thick consistency. Allow to cool slightly, taste, and add more sugar or vinegar if necessary to give a balanced sweet-and-sour flavour. Keep the sauce warm over a low heat until required.

Cut the soaked mushrooms in half. Coat the halves with plain flour and shallow-fry in oil until brown. Set aside to drain on paper towels.

Stir-fry the rest of the vegetables in the same pan with a little water. Season to taste with salt, pepper and monosodium glutamate (if using), then add the prepared Chinese mushrooms and sweet-and-sour sauce. Fry all together for another minute or so then serve, with fresh coriander.

Spinach with Oyster Sauce

Rau Mong Toi Xao Sot Dau Hao

2–3 slices ginger, peeled
1 kg (2 lb) spinach, carefully washed and cleaned, then coarsely shredded
2 tablespoons vegetable oil
1 onion, thinly sliced

Sauce:
2 tablespoons condensed oyster sauce
4 tablespoons water
1 teaspoon sugar

Spinach cooked this way has a crisp, crunchy texture nd retains a high vitamin content.

Bring a large saucepan of water to the boil. Add the ginger and spinach. When the water returns to the boil, drain the spinach thoroughly and spread it out on a large ovenproof serving plate or dish. Keep the spinach warm until needed.

Heat the oil in a small frying pan, add the onion and fry for 8 to 10 minutes until dark brown and crisp.

Meanwhile, combine all the ingredients for the sauce in a small saucepan. Bring to the boil, lower the heat and simmer for 1 to 2 minutes.

Pour the sauce over the spinach, sprinkle with the onion and serve immediately.

Sautéed Aubergine

Ca Tim Xao

250 ml (8 fl oz) oil
1 large aubergine, peeled, halved and cut diagonally in thick slices
5 tablespoons chicken stock
1 tablespoon nuoc mam (fish gravy)
1 teaspoon soy sauce
¼ teaspoon monosodium glutamate (optional)
3 spring onions, green tops only, sliced, to serve

Heat the oil in a large saucepan, add the aubergine slices and deep-fry until golden. Remove the aubergine slices with a slotted spoon and drain carefully on paper towels.

Place the fried aubergine slices in a large frying pan with the chicken stock, nuoc mam, soy sauce and monosodium glutamate (if using). Mix all the ingredients together well.

Bring to the boil, lower the heat and simmer, shaking the pan and moving the slices of aubergine around occasionally, until all the liquid has evaporated. Sprinkle with green tops of spring onion and serve immediately.

Aubergine in Black Bean Sauce

Ca Tim Xao Tuong Hot Ten

250 ml (8 fl oz) vegetable oil
1 large aubergine, peeled, halved and cut diagonally in thick slices
3 cloves garlic, crushed
2 slices root ginger, peeled and shredded
2 spring onions, chopped
7 tablespoons chicken stock
⅓ teaspoon ground black beans
1 teaspoon soy sauce
½ teaspoon sugar
¼ teaspoon monosodium glutamate (optional)
1 teaspoon cornflour
2 teaspoons water

Heat the oil in a large saucepan, add the aubergine slices and deep-fry until golden in colour. Remove the

Left: Spinach with Oyster Sauce; right: Sautéed Aubergine

aubergine slices with a slotted spoon and drain carefully on paper towels.

While the aubergine slices are draining, transfer 2 tablespoons of the oil from the saucepan to a large frying pan. Heat gently.

Add the crushed garlic and the shredded ginger to the frying pan and stir-fry in the oil for 2 to 3 minutes until the garlic is light golden in colour.

Add the fried aubergine slices to the pan with the chopped spring onions, stock, black beans, soy sauce, sugar and monosodium glutamate (if using). Mix all the ingredients together well and stir.

Bring to the boil, lower the heat and simmer for 1 to 2 minutes, stirring occasionally to prevent the mixture sticking to the pan.

Combine the cornflour and water in a cup. Mix carefully to a cream. Add to the aubergine mixture and cook, stirring constantly, until the sauce has thickened somewhat.

Serve immediately.

53

Left: Tomatoes Stuffed with Pork; right: Stir-fried Bamboo Shoot and Chinese Mushrooms

Tomatoes Stuffed with Pork

Thit Heo Don Ca

6 large tomatoes
300 g (11 oz) minced pork
4 tablespoons chopped canned water chestnuts
2 shallots, chopped
2 cloves garlic, crushed
2 tablespoons nuoc mam (fish gravy)
⅓ teaspoon freshly ground black pepper
1 teaspoon salt
2 tablespoons cornflour
pinch of monosodium glutamate (optional)
4 tablespoons vegetable oil
2 tablespoons chopped fresh parsley or coriander,
to serve

Cut each tomato in half horizontally, then squeeze out the seeds and scoop out most of the tomato pulp. Place the tomatoes upside down on paper towels to drain for at least 10–15 minutes.

Combine the remaining ingredients except the oil and parsley in a large bowl and mix together very thoroughly. Fill each tomato shell with the seasoned pork and water chestnut mixture.

Heat the oil in a large frying pan and add the tomatoes, stuffed-side down. Cook over gentle heat for about 15 minutes or until the tomatoes are soft and the filling has browned.

Carefully invert the tomatoes (so that the stuffed-side now faces up), on a heatproof platter and place under a preheated moderate grill for 10 minutes. Sprinkle with the parsley or coriander and serve immediately.

54

Stir-fried Bamboo Shoot and Chinese Mushrooms

Mang Xao Nam Dong Co

25 g (1 oz) dried Chinese mushrooms
4 tablespoons oil
2 slices root ginger, peeled
100 g (4 oz) piece bamboo shoot, thinly sliced
150 ml (¼ pint) chicken stock
1 tablespoon nuoc mam (fish gravy)
½ teaspoon salt
½ teaspoon sugar
1 teaspoon cornflour
1 tablespoon water

Place the dried mushrooms in a small bowl. Add warm water to cover and set aside for 15 minutes. Drain thoroughly. Discard stems and cut mushroom caps in half.

Heat the oil in a wok or large frying pan, add the ginger and stir-fry for 1 minute to extract the flavour. Add the bamboo shoot and reserved mushrooms and stir-fry for 1 to 2 minutes.

Add the stock and season with nuoc mam, salt and sugar. Mix well.

Bring to the boil, lower the heat and simmer for 2 minutes, stirring constantly.

Combine the cornflour and water in a cup and mix to a cream. Add to the stir-fry and cook, stirring constantly, until the sauce thickens. Serve immediately.

Chinese Mushrooms with Lemon Grass

Nam Dong Co Xao Xa

3 large pieces of bean curd
oil for deep frying
4 tablespoons vegetable oil
1 onion. coarsely chopped
1 stem of lemon grass, finely chopped
200 g (7 oz) dried Chinese mushrooms, soaked in water, drained and sliced
1 tablespoon light soy sauce
pinch of sugar
pinch of monosodium glutamate (optional)
3 tablespoons ground roasted peanuts
a large dish of assorted fresh leaves, such as those of cos lettuce, mint, coriander and basil, to serve

Cut the large pieces of bean curd into dice. Heat the oil in a deep-fat fryer or wok, add the bean curd dice then fry until golden brown, Drain and set aside.

Heat the vegetable oil in a large frying pan over a moderate heat and stir-fry the onion until golden brown. Add the lemon grass, prepared Chinese mushrooms and bean curd dice. Season with the soy sauce, sugar and monosodium glutamate (if using). Stir-fry gently for another 2 minutes. Serve hot, sprinkled with the peanuts. Eat with the assorted fresh leaves.

Steamed Bean Curd Paste

Dau Hu Hap

4 large pieces of bean curd
20 g (¾ oz) dried bean curd
20 g (¾ oz) cellophane noodles
1 teaspoon salt and pepper, mixed
½ teaspoon monosodium glutamate (optional)
1 tablespoon vegetable oil

Tomato sauce:
½ tablespoon cornflour
3 tablespoons water
1 teaspoon tomato purée
½ teaspoon salt

Blanch the large pieces of bean curd with hot water. Drain and leave to dry. Soak the dried bean curd and noodles in water for 30 minutes, then chop finely.

Meanwhile, make the tomato sauce. Mix all the ingredients together in a small saucepan and blend well, then bring to the boil, stirring constantly. Cook for 2 minutes over a low heat.

Mash the large pieces of bean curd in a bowl with a fork. Add all the other ingredients and mix well. Transfer this paste to an earthenware pot, then cover with a piece of cling film. Steam for 15 minutes. Remove the bean curd paste from the pot and put it on a warmed plate to serve. Reheat the tomato sauce if necessary, then pour it over the bean curd paste. Serve immediately.

Vietnamese Green Salad

Rau Tron

1 large lettuce
mint leaves
coriander leaves
1 cucumber

Separate the lettuce leaves and pile in the centre of a serving dish, then place the mint and coriander leaves in separate piles around the lettuce.

Peel the cucumber in thin strips to give an attractively variegated finish, then cut the cucumber in half. Remove all the seeds and cut into thin, half-moon-shaped slices. Place them, overlapping, around the edge of the dish. Serve the salad immediately.

55

Meduse Salad

Nom Sua

225 g (8 oz) dried meduse
2 cucumbers, halved and thinly sliced
6 carrots, thinly sliced or shredded
3 xu hao (kohlrabi), thinly sliced or shredded
1 tablespoon salt
120 ml (4 fl oz) water
2 cooked boneless chicken breasts, shredded
1 tablespoon fresh mint leaves
4 tablespoons nuoc mam giam, or to taste (see
Crispy Spring Rolls, page 14)

To serve:
2 tablespoons ground roasted peanuts
prawn crackers

Place the meduse in a large bowl with warm water to cover. Set aside for 15 minutes, then drain thoroughly. Rinse with boiling water, drain, then spread out to dry.

Meanwhile, place all the vegetables in a large mixing bowl. Add the salt and measured water and allow to stand for 15 minutes, occasionally pressing and squeezing the brine into the vegetables. Drain thoroughly.

Place a small amount of the prepared vegetables on a clean tea towel, roll the tea towel around the mixture and squeeze tightly to extract all the moisture. Repeat until all the vegetables are dry.

Transfer the vegetables to a serving bowl.

Cut the soaked and dried meduse into 5 cm (2 inch) lengths and add to the bowl, together with the chicken and mint leaves. Stir in 2 tablespoons nuoc mam giam, adding the rest only if required. Mix all the ingredients thoroughly, sprinkle with roasted peanuts and serve immediately, with prawn crackers.

Shredded Chicken Salad

Goi Ga

½ large white cabbage, finely shredded and cut in
4 cm (1½ inch) lengths
2 teaspoons salt
2 tablespoons lemon juice
1 tablespoon chopped fresh coriander leaves
1 tablespoon chopped fresh mint leaves
2 tablespoons nuoc mam giam (see Crispy Spring
Rolls, page 14)
2 boneless chicken breasts, cooked and shredded
1½ tablespoons ground roasted peanuts, to serve

Place the shredded cabbage in a large bowl with the salt, lemon juice and water to cover. Set aside for 15 minutes. Drain thoroughly, squeezing the cabbage in clean hands to extract as much liquid as possible.

Transfer to a large bowl and add the coriander and mint. Mix well. Stir in the nuoc mam giam.

Pile the mixture on a large platter, top with the chicken, sprinkle with ground roasted peanuts and serve immediately.

Beef and Vegetable Salad

Thit Bo Gia Loi Chai

225 g (8 oz) rump steak, cut into thin slices
150 ml (5 fl oz) wine or cider vinegar
225 g (8 oz) fresh honeycomb tripe
450 ml (¾ pint) milk and water, mixed
½ mooli or icicle radish, peeled and thinly sliced
225 g (8 oz) bean sprouts, trimmed
2 stems lemon grass, thinly sliced
1 red pepper, seeded and cut into fine strips
1 small onion, peeled and sliced
a few leaves of Cos Lettuce, shredded

Salad sauce:
3 garlic cloves, unpeeled
3 shallots, unpeeled
1 piece of root ginger or rhizome, peeled and chopped
2 tablespoons nuoc mam (fish gravy)
brown sugar
lime juice
6 tablespoons ground roasted peanuts

Place the steak in a shallow dish and cover with the vinegar. Marinate for 30 minutes, then remove the steak, drain and dry with paper towels. Reserve the marinade.

Cook the tripe in the milk-and-water mixture for 45 minutes or until tender to the knife. Drain and cut into thin slices.

Next make the sauce. Grill the garlic and shallots. Cool, then peel. Pound with the ginger using a pestle and mortar. Add this to the reserved marinade, then heat gently for 2 minutes. Add the fish sauce, then add sugar and lime juice to taste. Add 4 tablespoons of the ground roasted peanuts, stir well, then thin with a little water.

Mix the slices of beef and tripe with the prepared mooli, bean sprouts and lemon grass. Season to taste, then arrange on a platter. Sprinkle with the remaining peanuts, the strips of red pepper and the slices of onion. Arrange the lettuce around the edge of the platter. Serve immediately with the sauce.

Left: Shredded Chicken Salad; right: Meduse Salad

57

Desserts

Desserts are not an important feature of Vietnamese cooking. The major reason for this is that sweet flavours are integral to the taste of Vietnamese meat and fish dishes, and so the palate has no need of further sweetening after the main dishes are finished. The ten recipes included in this short chapter do, though, give the reader some idea of the kind of desserts enjoyed in Vietnam: light, tasty, refreshing sweets, mostly based on fruit. As ever, the aesthetic element is prominent, most notably here in the use of crushed ice as a background on which to present the food.

Banana and Pineapple Fritters

Chuoi Va Thom Chien Gion

oil for deep-frying
4 bananas
4 pineapple rings, fresh or canned
icing sugar, sieved, to coat

Batter:
50 g (2 oz) self-raising flour
150 g (5 oz) plain flour
¼ teaspoon baking powder
pinch of salt
1½–2 teaspoons vegetable oil
water (see method)
1 egg white, stiffly beaten

Prepare the batter. Combine the flours, baking powder, salt and oil in a large bowl. Stir in enough water to form a smooth paste. Lightly fold in the stiffly beaten egg white.

Heat the oil in a deep-fat fryer.

Meanwhile, peel the bananas and cut them in half lengthways. Drain the pineapple rings on paper towels to remove excess juice or syrup.

Quickly dip the fruit into the batter and cook in batches in the hot oil until puffed and golden. Do not add too many fritters to the pan at any one time, or the temperature of the oil will fall and the results will be unsatisfactory.

Drain the cooked fritters on paper towels, sprinkle with sieved icing sugar and serve immediately while still hot.

Variation: Thick apple rings may be used instead of banana or pineapple, if preferred, or any other firm fruit, fresh or tinned, provided it is well drained.

Agar Agar Jelly

Thach

10 g (¼ oz) agar agar strands
water (see method)
6 tablespoons sugar
5 drops banana essence
crushed ice
slices of starfruit (carambolas) to serve

Place the agar agar strands in a bowl. Add cold water to cover and set aside for at least 1 hour.

Meanwhile, combine 5 tablespoons of the sugar with 250 ml (8 fl oz) water in a small saucepan. Bring to the boil, stirring until all the sugar has dissolved. Boil

Left: Banana and Pineapple Fritters; right: Agar Agar Jelly

steadily, without stirring, for 2 minutes, then add 3 drops of banana essence and set aside to cool.

Drain the agar agar strands and place them in a saucepan with 600 ml (1 pint) water. Bring to the boil, lower the heat and simmer, stirring constantly until all the agar agar has dissolved. Stir in the remaining sugar and banana essence. Pour into a shallow baking tray and allow to cool, then refrigerate until quite firm.

When the agar agar jelly is solid, cut it into julienne (matchstick) strips. Half fill 4 tall serving glasses with jelly strips, top with crushed ice and add 2 to 3 teaspoons of the banana syrup to each glass. Mix well and decorate with slices of starfruit.

Bananas in Coconut Milk

Chuoi Dua

3 tablespoons tapioca
8 firm bananas
600 ml (1 pint) coconut milk (see Steamed Eel, page 23)
palm sugar or demerara sugar to taste
¼ teaspoon vanilla essence
1–2 tablespoons ground roasted peanuts to serve

Bring a saucepan of water to the boil, add the tapioca and cook, stirring constantly until the tapioca clears. Drain in a colander, rinse thoroughly and set aside.

Peel the bananas and cut into quarters. Place in a heavy-bottomed saucepan with the coconut milk. Add sugar to taste and cook over low heat, stirring constantly, until thick and creamy. Stir in the vanilla essence. Serve hot, sprinkled with peanuts.

60

Fruit Salad Ice Mountain

Chilled Avocado with Condensed Milk

Bo Tron Sua

4 ripe avocados
crushed ice
4 tablespoons condensed milk

This dessert is best prepared just before serving so that the avocado flesh does not discolour it. It is quick and easy to prepare.

Halve the avocados, discard the stones and place the flesh in a bowl. Mash well or purée in a food processor or blender.

Half fill 4 tall serving glasses with avocado purée, add crushed ice to within 4 cm (1½ inches) of the top and mix well. Top each glass with 1 tablespoon of condensed milk and serve.

Each guest mixes the condensed milk into his or her avocado ice before eating. Condensed milk is already sweetened, but extra sugar may be added.

Fruit Salad Ice Mountain

Hoa Qua Tuoi

1 small watermelon
1 papaya
1 × 312 g (11 oz) can lychees
1 × 454 g (16 oz) can longans
1 × 454 g (16 oz) can jack fruit
3 bananas
100 g (4 oz) fresh dates
2 tablespoons seedless raisins
crushed ice

Syrup:
225 g (8 oz) sugar
350 ml (12 fl oz) water

To serve:
fresh mint leaves
whipping cream

This is one of the simplest of Vietnamese desserts, and it is also one of the most refreshing and pleasing to the eye. For the best results, both fruit and syrup must be very cold.

First make the syrup. Combine the sugar and water in a small heavy-bottomed saucepan. Bring to the boil, stirring constantly until all the sugar has dissolved. Boil steadily, without stirring, for 2 minutes. Remove from the heat and set aside. When cool, refrigerate until required.

Prepare the fruit. Cut the watermelon in half, discard the seeds and cut the flesh into cubes or rounds. Transfer to a large bowl. Add the papaya, prepared in the same way. Drain the lychees, longans and jack fruit and cut the jack fruit into quarters. Slice the bananas. Stir all these fruits into the bowl together with the dates

and raisins. Chill all the fruit in the refrigerator until required.

Just before serving, pile crushed ice in the centre of a large platter to make a miniature ice mountain. Decorate with the fruit salad, then decorate carefully with fresh mint leaves. Trickle cold syrup over the top of the mountain and serve with the remaining syrup in a small jug, and the cream, whipped if desired.

Bean and Kiwi Fool

Che Dau Dong Lanh

225 g (8 oz) mung beans, rinsed, then soaked in cold
water overnight
150 ml (¼ pint) milk
300 ml (½ pint) double cream
50 g (2 oz) brown sugar, or to taste
2 tablespoons sake or medium-dry sherry
½ teaspoon vanilla essence
2 kiwi fruit, peeled and mashed
1 kiwi fruit, peeled and sliced, to serve

Drain the beans, then rinse thoroughly under cold running water. Place in a large saucepan and cover with fresh cold water. Bring to the boil, half-cover the pan with the lid, then lower the heat and simmer for 45 minutes to 1 hour, adding more water if necessary, until the beans are soft and tender. Drain thoroughly.

Put the beans in a food processor and work to a purée. Add the milk and half of the cream and stir to make a thick, batter-like consistency, then add the sugar, sake or medium-dry sherry and vanilla essence. Pour into individual glasses or a large bowl, cover and chill in the refrigerator.

When you are ready to serve, spread the mashed kiwi fruit evenly on top of the dessert. Whip the remaining cream until thick, then spoon over the top of the kiwi fruit purée. Finish by decorating with slices of kiwi fruit.

Corn Pudding

Che Bap

500 g (1¼ lb) corn-on-the-cob, uncooked
1 litre (1¾ pints) water
100 g (4 oz) glutinous rice, uncooked weight
300 g (11 oz) sugar
small pinch of salt
200 ml (7 fl oz) coconut milk
cream or coconut cream, to serve

Grate the uncooked corn-on-the-cob on a grater, then discard the cobs. Place the grated corn in a saucepan with the water and glutinous rice, then bring to the boil. Partially cover the saucepan and simmer gently until the grains of rice are broken and soft.

Stir in the sugar bit by bit, tasting as you do so: you may not want to use it all. Mix well, and add the pinch of salt. Remove from the heat, then stir in the coconut milk. Mix well again.

Serve hot, topped with cream or coconut cream.

Mung Bean Pudding

Che Dau Xanh

*225 g (8 oz) yellow mung beans, picked over
and washed
4 tablespoons tapioca
100 g (4 oz) sugar, or to taste
½ teaspoon vanilla essence
double cream or coconut milk to serve*

Soak the mung beans in cold water to cover for 6 to 8 hours, preferably overnight.

Next day, drain the beans and transfer them to a heavy-bottomed saucepan. Add water to 5 cm (2 inches) above the beans. Bring to the boil, lower the heat and simmer for 20 to 30 minutes until the beans are soft.

Meanwhile, bring a saucepan of water to the boil, add the tapioca and cook, stirring constantly, until the tapioca clears. Drain in a colander, rinse thoroughly and set aside.

Drain the beans and purée while still hot in a food processor or blender.

Return the purée to the clean saucepan, add water to just cover and bring to the boil. Lower the heat and simmer, stirring steadily for 2 minutes. Stir in the sugar, reserved tapioca and vanilla essence and simmer, stirring until the mixture is smooth. It should have the consistency of creamy porridge. If it is too thick add more water, 1 tablespoon at a time. Check the sweetness of the mixture, and add 1 or 2 extra tablespoons of sugar if felt necessary.

Serve hot or cold, topped with cream or coconut milk.

Mung Bean and Sesame Cakes

Dau Xanh Vung

Filling:
*100 g (4 oz) yellow mung beans
175 ml (6 fl oz) water
100 g (4 oz) sugar*

Wrapping:
*225 g (8 oz) glutinous rice flour
1 teaspoon baking powder
½ teaspoon salt
100 g (4 oz) sugar
2 medium-sized potatoes, boiled, peeled and
mashed
120 ml (4 fl oz) boiling water*

To finish:
*50 g (2 oz) sesame seeds
oil for deep frying*

First make the filling. Rinse the mung beans thoroughly under cold running water. Put the beans and the water in a saucepan and bring to the boil. Lower the heat, cover and simmer for about 30 minutes, or until the beans have absorbed all the water and are tender and dry. Remove from the heat and mash the beans, then add the sugar and mix well.

Make the wrapping next. Put all the ingredients except the boiling water in a bowl. Mix well, then gradually stir in the boiling water. Knead the mixture until it forms a smooth ball.

Roll 2 tablespoons of the wrapping mixture into a small ball, then flatten into a 7.5 cm (3 inch) circle. Place 1 teaspoon of the filling mixture in the centre of the circle and gather the wrapping together to enclose the filling, shaping it into a ball. Repeat with the remaining wrapping and filling mixture until all the ingredients are used up (the mixtures should be enough for about 12 balls). Set aside.

Heat a heavy frying pan until very hot. Add the sesame seeds and stir-fry in the dry pan until well-browned. (It is essential to use a very hot pan for this or the seeds will become oily and not stick to the dough.)

Put the toasted sesame seeds on a plate or a piece of greaseproof paper and roll the balls in the seeds until completely coated.

Deep-fry the cakes in hot oil, a few at a time, for about 10 minutes or until golden brown and cooked. Remove and drain carefully on paper towels, then serve while still warm

Banana Cake

Banh Chuoi

*6 bananas
200 ml (7 fl oz) water
200 ml (7 fl oz) coconut milk
200 g (7 fl oz) plain flour
100 g (4 oz) sugar
single cream (optional), to serve*

Peel the bananas and cut them into 10 mm thick rounds. Put them into the saucepan with the water. Bring the water and bananas to the boil and then simmer until the water has reduced to a quarter of its original volume. Set aside to cool.

Mix the coconut milk with the plain flour and the sugar. Add the reduced banana-and-water mixture to this, then stir all together thoroughly.

Pour the mixture into an earthenware container and steam it in the top part of a steamer for 30 minutes. Serve hot or cold, with single cream if desired.